Praise

The Rediscovery of Hope and Purpose

Written during a time of uncertainty, this book offers lessons on making the world a better place through hope and service. Christopher Albrecht mines stories from his own life, his career as a teacher, and interviews with people from around the world to illuminate the power of maintaining hope in the face of doubt and fear. He brings these memorable stories to life and weaves them into an optimistic vision of what ordinary people can accomplish.
Sydney Chaffee, 2017 National Teacher of the Year

As an educator, Albrecht understands the profound importance of connecting our daily work with our hope for the future—and in helping us recognize a deeper purpose that not only reveals our personal values and passions, but also provides us an internal compass for a lifetime. The Rediscovery of Hope and Purpose takes us on a quest, and we encounter the wisdom of many others along the way. As Albrecht explores the accomplishments of historical figures, contemporary interviews with acclaimed individuals, and his own personal reflections, he provides a series of signposts to guide our journey—and perhaps to rediscover an eternal path waiting to be found again. As he says in the book, "Hope is never gained; it exists waiting to be recognized."
Craig Martin, Educator and Executive Director of Pegasus Springs Education Collective

In his book, Christopher Albrecht shows how we can draw inspiration and hope from others. The people he interviews and writes about remind us that we, too, can achieve fantastic things even in the face of great adversity and uncertainty. A positive, encouraging, and inspirational read that is perfectly suited for our modern time, The Rediscovery of Hope and Purpose will challenge you to be the best person that you can be.
Jacob Cianci-Gaskill, Ph.D.,
Biologist, University of Missouri

Christopher Albrecht asks the question, "Can one person change the world?" and proceeds to answer it through insightful interviews. His natural curiosity and gift for teaching through example shine through in this down to earth and very personal ode to "hope and purpose."

Betty Belanus, Ph.D., Education Specialist, Curator & Folklorist, Smithsonian Institution

I admire Chris' devotion to teaching and learning, whether in the classroom or through talking to all sorts of people with stories to tell. This book is no exception. He strives to learn all he can and to pass that knowledge onto others. With this book, he's educating about hope in all its forms, which is something we desperately need in the world right now.

Kate Auletta, Senior Editor, Culture & Parenting, HuffPost

Albrecht argues convincingly that hope always has rested inside each of us, waiting to be melded with our life's purpose in ways that can be life changing. Using story, humor, and intelligent in-depth interviews, he explores the nature of hope, its power, even its limitations, reminding us it is the driving force behind our growth and our future. A great read!

Judi Knipmeyer, Vice President, Fields of Dreams Uganda Board of Directors

Christopher has penned this book at a time when humanity needs hope and a sense of renewed purpose. He provides a welcome read for educators who wish to make a difference in this world. For those who wish to linger with a text and ponder possibility, this book is for you.

Dr. Dale-Elizabeth Pehrsson, President, Clarion University of Pennsylvania

There's something about Christopher Albrecht that just makes you dream big. It's what makes him an excellent teacher, and unsurprisingly, translates just as seamlessly in _The Rediscovery of_

Hope and Purpose. Albrecht uses a blend of unedited interviews and personal narratives gives the reader a "roadmap" to rediscovering hope and purpose at a time when many of us could use it the most. _The Rediscovery of Hope and Purpose_ will make you smile, laugh and maybe even cry as you navigate that roadmap and dare to dream big.
Ryann Brooks, The Emporia Gazette

This book will make you smile. Most of all, it will make you hope again. In a time when all we seem to experience is one crisis after another, this book brims with the effervescent humor, wit, and wisdom of a great fourth grade teacher! It will be a book you will recommend to friends.
Fr. David B. Couturier, OFM, Executive Director, Franciscan Institute, St. Bonaventure University

The dreamers and seekers captured in these pages have charted new, often unexpected territory for themselves, and in doing so, provide a reminder that a spirit of exploration and self-discovery can lead out into a world that is waiting for what each of us has to offer. In this time calling out for the light of hope and a strength of purpose, these lively, surprising conversations serve as reminders of what life can be when we strive to live into our authentic selves. Christopher Albrecht, with his abiding curiosity and a life-long habit of looking at the world with eyes of wonder, has gathered stories reminding us that what is rooted in adversity can be grounded in joy.
Linda Cloutier-Namdar, Educator,
2018 Vermont Teacher of the Year

We at 261 Fearless have long known that hope and purpose are our eternal fires, but we all need to take the first step to discover them. Just as surely as someone helps us take the first tentative step out the door and watches as we eventually run a marathon, The Rediscovery of Hope and Purpose, gives us all that First Fearless Step.
261 Fearless, Inc., Non-Profit, Empowering Women Globally Through Running and Education

Christopher Albrecht's second book builds on the premise of the need for a roadmap for rediscovering two essential elements in meaningful human existence: hope and purpose. While not conforming to any known genre of literature, this book is compelling and insightful with personal narratives, family bonding, and sensitive interviews that force the reader to reflect, analyze, be inspired to be a little better, give a little more, and not lose the true essence of our time on earth. If the pandemic has taught us nothing else, it has pointed us toward those things that help us look for that rainbow or that one shining star amid the darkness. Albrecht's book is that guiding star for me. Hope, Purpose, and Albrechtism-- what we all need right now, more than ever!
Carol Strickland,
Executive Director, National Teachers Hall of Fame

At a time in history when hope has often felt fragile, let Christopher Albrecht remind you just how strong it is. Via compelling interviews with extraordinary individuals, Albrecht's The Rediscovery of Hope and Purpose brings readers along with him on an uplifting journey of self-discovery. Sprinkled in are anecdotes from Albrecht's own remarkable trek from a son of immigrants and first-generation college student to the 2018 New York State Teacher of the Year.
Caurie Putnam-Ferguson,
Journalist -Reuters and the USA Today Network

The Rediscovery of Hope and Purpose offers a thoughtful, timely, and empowering message that will benefit all readers. Through Christopher Albrecht's poignant personal narrative, beautifully interwoven with the stories and perspectives of individuals who understand the value and the power of hope, readers will be moved by the heartfelt insights, powerful experiences, and meaningful outlooks on life presented throughout this book. In the midst of these challenging times, Christopher's biographical sketches, and personal recollections offer strategies, ideas, opportunities for self-reflection, and other considerations for a better tomorrow.
David Bosso, Ed.D., Educator, 2012 Connecticut Teacher of the Year, 2019 National Teachers Hall of Fame Inductee

Assisted by an eclectic mix of world-changing people, award-winning educator Christopher Albrecht provides us with a fascinating lesson plan on how to rediscover the hope and purpose lurking within each of us. Whether it's a barrier-breaking woman marathoner, a world-renown landscape photographer, a 104-year-old children's author, a Seinfeld writer and producer, or a national champion football coach, we learn through example and introspection the essentials for living a truly meaningful life. Albrecht does a masterful job of asking thought-provoking questions and weaving in his own experiences and perspectives. After reading this inspirational book, it's easy to see why he has received lofty recognition for teaching his students lessons that last a lifetime.
Scott Pitoniak,
Nationally Honored Journalist and Best-Selling Author

Ranging across woodworking, soccer, the symbiotic relationship between plants and fungi, and the importance of storytelling, <u>The Rediscovery of Hope and Purpose</u> expands our understanding of hope and resilience, of the necessary combination of passion and pain. Christopher Albrecht is a teacher—a word that hardly encompasses what he does in the classroom and in this book. He helps his readers to see, as he says, "The path to hope and purpose starts with an uphill run." Combining stories of the well-known and the lesser known, Albrecht tells the story of empowerment: of women and girls, of immigrants, of college presidents, and most poignantly of his father. Near the end of the book, Albrecht notes: "Teaching is a lot like putting a jigsaw puzzle together. Inspiration is analogous to attaching two adjoining pieces of a puzzle. Satisfaction is when two pieces finally fit." This book is a jigsaw puzzle, too, and one that fits: if the reader is willing to take time to learn the lessons in it and make a commitment to hope. I am a richer person for having read it.
Dr. Heidi Macpherson,
President, SUNY College at Brockport

Also by Christopher Albrecht
Unconventionally Successful

Unconventionally Successful (NFB Publishing, Buffalo, NY) is the first book released from a broad grassroots project Christopher Albrecht (2018 New York State Teacher of the Year & 2019 Inductee into the National Teachers Hall of Fame) has published, which uncovers what best practices schools, individuals, and communities need to consider to increase their levels of success. People want our world to be full of successful journeys and results. This book sheds light on many unconventional and potentially unconsidered out of the box thoughts and actions that led to extraordinary outcomes. Entertaining and informative, this novel binds three formats: interview, reflection, and narrative. Albrecht spent three years interviewing hundreds people from diverse backgrounds and lifestyles asking them to reflect on their recollections, memories and experiences with teachers and their many impacts on their lives. Focused around eight interviews, the author parallels research on similar historical narratives and reflections. The result is a one of a kind read that uncovers unconventional patterns, unique circumstances, and opportunities, which light the road of joy and happiness that root themselves in our schools and colleges. The patterns Albrecht has discovered and shares in this groundbreaking book have the potential for lifelong effects and impacts on the success of individuals, communities, schools, and the world we live in that are not explicitly obvious. This book is a must-read for all people who enjoy discovering non-linear, unique and creative pathes that lead to innovative ways individuals and groups have found happiness, joy and success.

THE REDISCOVERY OF HOPE AND PURPOSE

Awakening the Human Spirit

Christopher W. Albrecht

NFB Publishing
Buffalo, New York

Copyright © 2021 Christopher W. Albrecht

Printed in the United States of America

THE REDISCOVERY OF HOPE AND PURPOSE:
Awakening the Human Spirit/ Albrecht— 1st Edition

ISBN: 978-1-953610-19-5

> 1. Title.
> 2. Spirtituality/Self-Improvement
> 3. Philosophy.
> 4. Interviews.
> 5. Albrecht.
> 6. Investigative Social Philosophy.

No part of this book may be reproduced or transmitted in any form by any means, electronic or mechanical, including photocopying, recording, or by any information storage and retrieval system without permission in writing by the author.

For more information about the author visit:
Website: christopheralbrecht.com
Twitter: @Albrecht_NYSTOY
Facebook: facebook.com/Christopher.albrecht.37

NFB
NFB Publishing/Amelia Press
119 Dorchester Road
Buffalo, New York 14213

For more information visit Nfbpublishing.com

To my father, Werner August Albrecht

... and a much older dog named Harley, who sleeps a lot more,
but still warms my feet late at night while I write.

Table of Contents

Foreword   I

The First Light of Hope   IX

Chapter 1 - Carve the Unnecessary
Distractions Out of Your Life   1

Chapter 2 - All Chips In   18

Chapter 3 - Purpose in Poverty   42

Chapter 4 - Share the Mountains
That People Can't Climb   65

Chapter 5 - One Lives When One Fails   81

Chapter 6 - Keep Your Brain
Open for Business   106

Chapter 7 - Free is the Price of Hard Work   128

Chapter 8 - Hope is Self-Serving
When Serving Others   143

Chapter 9 - Talent Has a Flat Distribution,
Opportunity Does Not   166

Chapter 10 - Jumpman Changed the World   187

Chapter 11 - Coming to America   209

One Final Thought   226

About the Author   231

FOREWORD

IN MARCH OF 2020, a letter arrived in my mailbox. It was from my father. At the time, my dad was eighty-four years old and a German citizen. He was born in 1935—a child of bombings, occupations, poverty, starvation, and a lack of schooling. Yet the letter arrived in the most pristine cursive, with perfect spelling and voice.

I am a fourth-grade teacher. When this letter showed up, I had morphed into an online educator who was stitching seams of my hot air balloon as it was leaving Earth. Technology was all new to me, and entirely counter-productive to kinesthetic learning. Typing on a keyboard is not movement, at least by the standards of a normal fourth-grade classroom. Fourth graders are not meant to stay in chairs for extended periods of time. I was stuck. Using a computer means sitting, looking, and listening. There is not a whole lot of moving going on. I was virtually holding online office hours with eight- and nine-year-old students because a swift and mysterious virus had come out of a valley in China that few Americans had ever heard of, and now the world was on its heels. It took the leash off human nature in many, leaving their greed unchecked. People were waiting at 6:00 AM in cold rain for the supermarkets to open their doors with the next stocking of necessities: pasta, milk, bread, and... toilet paper. Items were being over-purchased, leaving little for others. Panic was setting in and distracting rational thought with the authority of a cop at an intersection. Just three months earlier, the economy of the United States blistered to one of the greatest growth surges in history over a three-year period. Within weeks, that was erased, and people were imprisoned in their houses and apartments because of the fear of catching this enigmatic virus that was now beginning to claim lives by the hundreds per day. People were petrified.

The pandemic crippled my profession. My life as a teacher was not changing day to day, but hour by hour. In 2020, I was in my 25th year of teaching. I was also a second-year adjunct professor at a local college. Up to this point, I was well below average with my understanding of technology, computers, gadgets, and networks. In a mean twist of fate, I began my career in a job I did not ever intend to pursue. I started as a technology teacher on the heels of the advent of the internet, but I quickly shifted to elementary education. I returned to the safety of books, lined paper, and pencils. Innovation blazed by me, and I did not care. I had avoided technology at all costs. Know-how was confusing and it seemed like ideas came rapid-fire. For a guy who has worn the same shirt rotation for decades, change is not good. Rapid change makes me head for the hills and hide. Variations of applications were happening too fast for me, so instead of trying to fill the void of insecurity every day, I simply gave up. New websites were popping up all the time. I had no interest in them.

I am a creature of habit and stability. I email attachments. Up until the virus, that was the extent of my pioneering voyage into technological education. Sharing documents? Online voice chats? Message boards? Every time one of my colleagues brought up such foreign words at a meeting, I just smiled and nodded like I fully understood. I grasped none of it. Who knew how much a twenty-five-year career could change within a few days? In the blink of an eye, our school went from embracing the finals of the spelling bee to the governor of New York saying that we should not leave our homes. How could a virus take us prisoner? No school. No leaving the house. I had no choice. Hello, Mr. Computer. Help! My computer skills lean much closer to the smoke signal part of the bell-curve than that of an M.I.T. professor. I had to morph, and fast.

This book was imagined in the months leading up to the afore-mentioned distress, but the first words were written during the first modern global pandemic. Knowing that this moment in time was historic, I deviated from preset ideas only slightly to give readers years from now a firsthand account of what writing a book during an unprecedented event is like. However, if you are looking for a book about gloom and doom, put this one right back. The stage was grimly set, but this book has no zombie apoc-alypse or suspense. I promise you, as a man of strong hope, I only mention the pandemic because it will be talked about for years.

It was a Saturday in March. I have a strange habit that origi-nates from my significant other. I take my socks off in the garage, so I can walk barefoot to my mailbox. Perhaps it is a little weird, but so what? Putting on shoes feels like more effort than taking off my socks. I am a kid of the 1970s. We went barefoot every-where. Nike changed all that sometime in the early 80s. The hab-it never left. I flipped through the mail on the way back up my driveway. To my surprise there was a letter from my dad. Let me preface by saying that a letter from my father is rare, and when they do come, they have one of two things: a new AAA card or a recollection of something that happened years ago. Dad likes to tell stories, and he has clung on to paying for my AAA fees since I was in high school. However, beyond that, the letter speaks for itself.

Dear Christopher:

Klaus [his brother who was 86 years old at the time and lives in Germany] and I talked again as we so often do each week. His flu was bad this time, and so was Marianne's [my Uncle Klaus' wife]. He could not see her for a few days, and she understood it [she is in a nursing home]. He sounded better now—I was concerned a couple of days ago. We talked about the Corona 19 virus. They have the same problems over there [Germany]— people are nervous about it, they go shopping for food, empty shelves, etc. Here and there, in between, we talk about memories, old memories. Some he does not remember, the same with me. The toilet paper shortage is one thing which—for us—brought memories back from the war [World War II]. It's in my mind vividly. Muttle [his mother] cut small sheets from newspaper, about one-fourth of the width of a sheet of paper. It was on a wire string next to the toilet on a wall hook. Sometimes, it was cut just right, and you could read a short story, part of a story, naturally before the sheet was... Sometimes there was no newspaper available and "ersatz" had to be used.

Anyways, there came a time when Muttle had a splendid idea. No paper, just nothing, and there were five of us: Muttle, Katia, and the three of us. But, in Vatle's [his father's] study there was paper, many books. Muttle was resourceful—some of Vatle's books had to go. Vatle was far away, in Poland or Russia, or in a hospital in Northern Germany. He did not know about Muttle's using of the books or journals.

When he finally came home, the war was over, and things got better. But a new war was started: He found out, Muttle confessed that the books were sacrificed. Oh- Vatle was angry, all hell broke loose. But, after a while, it got better.

Weeks later, the man came with the ox cart. There was a large, long round barrel on the cart, and up on the top was an opening. On a stick, sort of a long broomstick was a small bucket, about a gallon. This was the version of a honey dipper of the 1930s and

40s. When the barrel was full, the ox pulled the cart to a field, the man pulled the spicket, the ox moved, and the field was fertilized with the pages of Vatle's books—gone, of course.
These were the good old days! Who ever thought of e-coli?

Love you!
Dad

Dad's memories were ignited by our modern pandemic. I have never lived through a world war and never want to. Chances are, if you are under the age of 85, neither have you. We are privileged. A toilet paper catastrophe seems like the end of the world. Maybe not.

This is a book about hope. My Christian education sledgehammered the three virtues of faith, hope, and love into me like a carpenter pounding nails into the wood structure of a house. The foundation for this novel comes from my observation of children. As I quote in my first book, Unconventionally Successful, "children are the dipstick of the health of a community." I work with eight-, nine-, and ten-year-old students all day. This year, with my partner teacher of twenty-two years, I served forty-eight students. After the economic mess of this spring settles, that number will most likely go up. Or, if the pandemic does not fade and social distancing becomes the new norm, who knows how much real estate each child will be allotted? Regardless, we have spent a lot of time teaching together with over a thousand children between us. There are a lot of moments where I am able to peer through a unique lens into our community's health. What do I see? Distractions—lots of distractions. The increase of objects, information, and noise that takes our mind off what is right in front of our noses correlates with a declining trend in the understanding and recognition of hope and purpose. The evidence can be found by asking anyone to define hope. You will get a lot of different answers. This trend was happening before the pandemic. My early notes say so.

Is all lost? Absolutely not. My motivation for writing this book is a lot like a doctor's prescription of an antibiotic for strep throat. My vision, which uncovers explicit examples of how we can lead healthier and more joyful lives by rediscovering hope and our purpose, is held in the following pages. All is not lost, and it never will be. But I feel like we are in a metaphorical winter freeze in which the word "hope" has been in an extended hibernation. Moving in the wrong direction is better than standing still. Stagnant water always fosters disease. It is the same way with life. We need to get on the same page. It is time to wake up the sleeping bear. Hope is the bear—powerful and confident. A bear walks with purpose.

When first outlining this book, I created eleven constructs that develop into hope. Then I went searching for people who not only understand the vision but are living it. The people that contributed are diverse: they are humble, quiet, loud, or philanthropic. Each person that shared in the construction of this book understands the implication of the rediscovery of hope and its widespread positive effect on humanity. I was fortunate to find ten people of wisdom, willing to impart their insight on hope. This book is a collection of the discussions I had with each person, brought together to give us a roadmap for the rediscovery of our hope and purpose. Paralleled and coupled with their insights are some reflections and short narratives. Hope has always been alive in every human being that has walked the Earth, but recognition of it can be a challenge. The discussions speak to the present, and the stories speak to our history. It is impossible to make progress if one is without the other. We are not all that different than those that walked the path before us.

Thank you for choosing to read this book. Welcome to your personal rediscovery of hope and purpose.

-Christopher

The First Light of Hope

PANDORA WAS CONCEIVED by the Greek god of fire, Hephaestus, and she held her moral values close to her heart. When she was created, she received many offerings. Aphrodite gave deep emotion, Hermes bequeathed a mastery of language, and Athena gifted craftsmanship, among other gifts from the gods. Pandora also received the gift of curiosity of the world around her, though the giver of curiosity changed depending on which version of the myth you read. In every version, however, Zeus bestowed the most crucial gift, a heavy, tightly closed jar or box. The contents of the box were not for mortal eyes, and she was told that she should never open it. As Pandora grew older, curiosity drew her back to the box. The enigma of the box became maddening. Moral values tugged her away from the box, but curiosity drew her in. Pandora was a lot like the kid who finds where Mom and Dad stashed the Christmas presents. Believing that she could just peek, she cracked the lid. Demons and horrors exploded out, filling the world with sadness, anger, and fear. Zeus had locked away all evil spirits in the box. Pandora released them, and everything changed.

The story of Pandora's box often stops there, and its legend has carried a lesson throughout history: *don't open Pandora's box.* The truncation of the myth of Pandora has warped the meaning of Pandora's box. There is more to the story.

As Pandora cowered and was frozen from fear, she heard a faint but peaceful sound echoing from the box. The sound caused her to tingle. Pandora peered in the box again, and light blazed forth. The illumination was that of hope, trapped along with all the evils of the world. Though Pandora could never recapture the evil that came from the box, hope came with all that was released.

Find a bathroom with a mirror. You are safe in the bathroom because the only witness will be you. Bathroom judgement is personal and private; it is a safe zone. Gaze into the mirror and consider how you are living your life. What do you see?

As a fourth-grade teacher, I know—as any *true* educator knows—that we all remain teachers when we leave the confines of our workspace. Teaching is a lifestyle, and sometimes I am the pesky mosquito of the group when I go into teacher mode. It happens regardless of age. My poor wife and kids live with it (pity them). Me? I love it because many years ago I discovered that it is not my job to stand in front of the classroom. The teaching space is designed to elevate students, and like the greatest umpires on a baseball field, I am meant to become nearly invisible. In the end, it is my sincerest hope that students come to understand that I am not a book of answers. I will live if my name fades over time. I do not have all the answers. My mission of hope is that within the confines of the 375 minutes per day that I have for the 186 days per year that I officially teach, my students learn what I consider the greatest lesson: *ask yourself and the person closest to you what he or she thinks*. More often than not, nine-year-old children have a better answer than I could come up with in a lifetime.

Are you still looking in the mirror? Whether you are happy with your life or not, you are a person of value. I know that not everybody knows or even believes this fact, but this is a self-evident truth. All people are worthy. Nobody on this Earth is without significance. Do you know your gift to the world? If you do not, ask yourself, because you are now awkwardly staring into a mirror, *what is my gift to the world? What do I owe myself? What can I do to make tomorrow an improvement on today?* I cannot tell you what each person's gift is. That is up to the individual. It is not vain, selfish, or wrong to admit what you have. Likewise, we must know our deficits. If your gift is simply a smile, that is fine. As you will find in this book, a smile may be all you need.

A year before my mother succumbed to ovarian cancer, I asked my family to write Mom questions. With a recorder, she imparted these words: *Success equals being happy with yourself.* If I feel over the course of my life I have discovered a few things that I believe will be beneficial to others, it is my duty to impart what I know and observe. This book is a roadmap toward the rediscovery of hope and purpose. It is not the only road, but I am identifying—at minimum—a highway. It is there dangling like a ripe garden tomato waiting to be picked, but if we do not know the path to the garden, we never taste sweet hope. The world always has and always will be hungry for hope. Successful people long for it and so do the destitute. The realization of that varies. YOU DESERVE TO HAVE HOPE!

I wish I could say that what you are about to discover comes in pill form. It would be so easy to pop medicine and be done with it. Not so. The rediscovery of hope is parallel to Homer's Odyssey. For some people, it means fighting your way out of hell but finding the realization that every climb up a mountain begins with one step. Take the first step! If you picked up this book looking for answers, put it down, and go back to the mirror. Like a fingerprint, your path to increasing the amount of hope in your life basket can only be filled by the person staring back at you. This book is a catalyst, but you must supply the fuel. You must trust yourself. Right now, break down all those barriers of doubt, mistakes, and pity. Be reassured that there are more people in the world like you than you think. Find comfort that every person alive feels these emotions. Suck it up, and contemplate that person in the mirror.

If you read this book, I promise you a mental overhaul—at minimum a tune up and validation, but potentially a rollercoaster ride and a very unconventional journey. Take a chance, a leap of faith, and read. You are headed on a crusade, a personal quest of sorts, to rediscover your own personal hope and purpose. I am going to guide you, but I am not anywhere near divine. I can only navigate. As captain, you must steer your personal ship. The personal answers you develop must come from within if they are going to fit your DNA perfectly. Hope takes a lifetime of commitment. What you will rediscover is what Pandora found at the bottom of the box—hope.

AND SO, WE BEGIN OUR JOURNEY...

CHRISTMAS EVE DINNER is the highlight of my father's year. I am an American; my father came to America in 1959 on a Pan Am 707. I learned this one Christmas. My father believes in saving family mementos. He writes stories about resurfacing memories tucked in the attic of his mind, and his reflections often arrive with a gift from the past. Dad was born in 1935, so he has seen a lot of change in the world. Each of us gets a snippet of time in history. We get what we get. Dad got a front row seat to World War II for his first ten years of life, but he does not talk about it resentfully. He understands that he got what he got. A memento accompanies all of Dad's stories. The memento is not store-bought, but a possession somewhere from the depths of his personal or family journey, collected and tucked away, that intersects with the narrative he has written.

About the time I turned forty, my Christmas present was not wrapped in traditional holiday paper. Instead, on Christmas Eve of 2012, my dad gave me an envelope. In it were two things. The first was his recollection of a flight on December 2nd, 1959 and what it was like to see the Statue of Liberty from the sky as he came to the United States for the first time. The second—tucked neatly between the pages—was the stub from the actual Pan Am ticket he held that day, monetarily worthless but historically irreplaceable. At the age of twenty-four, my father was going to go live in this foreign land called America. Both of his brothers were conformists. One went to college and became a German physicist and the other, a medical doctor. Dad was the youngest, the rebel, and like a master whittler with a pen knife, he carved his own path. He was headed to uncharted land, the United States of America.

My dad was not in a bathroom staring in a mirror. His reflection was clear in his mind. As a young German boy, he had lived through the Second World War. He witnessed occupations: French, Mongolian, British, and so on. Some stole because they could. Some raped because they could. The Americans brought chocolates and harmonicas because they could. The American occupation of his small town of Sulzbach built a curiosity and hope that grew from the flickers of a new fire to the blaze of a wildfire in his mind. In search of a better tomorrow, he had to come to America. He had a strong grasp of hope. My father looked at his life, saw what inspired him, and pursued it. He had little money and fewer possessions. Had these material distractions existed, they may have clouded his decisions, and he may never have followed his deep-rooted curiosity of living in America. Out of the ashes of World War II, he found hope in a new land. Dad came to America in 1959, and he never left.

To date, my father has lived in America for over sixty years and Germany for less than twenty-five, yet he has decided to remain a German citizen. The foundation of this book is based on a phenomenon I discovered through a series of letters from my father: the way that we discover and cultivate hope is to create mental roots that ground our identity. In my father's case, his discovery of hope happened in those years prior to coming to the United States, and they have forever caused him to identify himself as a German. Having discovered the hope that already existed within himself, my father was fortunate. Not everyone is. There is a growing population searching for the forested trail to their own rediscovery of hope. If you are one of them, know that you are not alone and very well could be in the majority.

My father's letters still randomly arrive, containing reflections about his memories and life experiences. Sometimes he gives me a story for my birthday or Christmas, but often, they arrive without reason with a memento from the past. Narratives about my Lutheran grandmother's strength during the Second World War have shown up with a pair of woolen socks she knitted in the 1940s. Another time he wrote about how my grandfather was stationed on the Russian front during the winter of 1942-1943. My grandfather risked execution by disobeying orders and helping poor Russian farmers who were starving, while record low temperatures froze the countryside outside of Moscow. A walking stick that a Russian carved in 1943 for my grandfather out of gratitude came with this story. His stories often reflect the good within the bad; the hope within the darkness; the bottom of Pandora's box. I peppered this book with a few of Dad's stories.

Hope can teach, but it often sits there staring a person right in the face going unrecognized and invisible. By sharing many unique life stories and interviews, my goal is that any person with an open mind will make a real connection within his or her life and see that there is hope that they may never have recognized on their own. We are surrounded by masters—people who walk among us that have beneficial insights. I was fortunate to have a father that continues to provide key insights on how to identify and develop hope and purpose.

During Dad's childhood, Christmas Eve was celebrated more than Christmas Day. This tradition carried over into my childhood, and now my father comes to our house every December 24th. For as far back as I can remember, my father has had a fascination with lottery scratch off tickets. Every Christmas Eve, right after the reading of Luke 3:16—a description of the birth of the Christ Child and the accounts of the shepherds on the hillside—our entire family moves our dinner plates away from their spots to find the traditional lottery scratch off ticket. The swirls of capitalism are deeply embedded within traditional Christian values. Some years when coins cannot be found, we scratch off our tickets with our best silverware.

Hope and wishes are two distinctly different matters. In a world that likes instant success and gratification, hopes and wishes have become twisted together. That tangled ball of yarn needs to be unwound. Unraveling knots is frustrating; it requires patience, observation, concentration, and above all, time. In a world full of wishes, it is so much easier to just throw out the yarn and buy a new ball of yarn at Walmart. Yarn is disposable, but people are not. The *throw out and start all over* mentality has been applied to people in a modern world, and the practice of the invalidation of human life is a key contributor to the erosion of hope. Every life has a knot. If humans are going to rediscover hope, people need to untie their own knots and avoid having others do it for them. We entangle the yarn because the path to hope is hard and an easy one to avoid. The rediscovery of hope and purpose takes grit.

Lottery tickets are wildly popular. Common sense says that the odds are stacked against everyone that plays. Whether a one-dollar or a twenty-dollar ticket is bought, the chances of revealing a ticket with a massive payout is slim. Why do people play? Why has my father created a tradition that most likely my kids will pass on to their kids? It screws up the Christmas spirit, right? Lotteries are all about capitalism. With each scratch, materialism stamps out all that we are supposed to strive for. Is the value of this yearly ritual about the wish of winning money? Should I stop it? Absolutely not. A lottery ticket is analogous to the unorthodox tradition of searching for a pickle hidden in the Christmas tree. Traditions give us hope and comfort. Scratching a lottery ticket on Christmas Eve is part of my family's thumbprint.

Everyone has a unique fingerprint associated with their life. Nobody before has ever lived the same life as you, and no one after will either. You are one of one. It is my hope that the following pages will put a figurative mirror in front of you, support your personal journey to the discovery of yourself, and in time, be the catalyst for your unique path to the rediscovery of hope and purpose.

CHAPTER 1
CARVE THE UNNECESSARY DISTRACTIONS OUT OF YOUR LIFE

"I took my Barlow knife and made my first one. It looked like it got into a horrible fight. So, I kept carving that summer."

-Chris Lubkemann

- 1 -

Before I was ten, I was obsessed with trying to read every page of the Guinness Book of World Records. Chris Lubkemann holds a Guinness Certificate for carving the world's smallest rooster with a Swiss Army knife. I taught his grandson, Isaac, in fourth grade. A few years after Isaac had moved to middle school, I received an email from Chris requesting to volunteer in my classroom for a day. I accepted; I can use all the help I can get. Little did I know that on the day he came, all my plans would go out the window. This man is one of one. He showed up in a van with a slingshot attached to the roof that he claimed could fire a baseball at 130 miles per hour! He and his interests are as unique as the clouds in the fall sky. Lubkemann has twisted a lifestyle, occupation, and hobby all into one by whittling twigs with a Swiss Army knife.

He is bold too. The day he came to school, he had me canceling all my activities so that my students could spend as much time with him as possible. Lubkemann has written five books on whittling wood with a pocketknife. In 2016, he was asked by Victorinox, the manufacturers of the Swiss Army knife, to write a book on whittling for their company. It now stands as the number one book in the world on the subject with 168,000 copies sold in its first three years. His story is one of hope. Like peeling the bark off wood, Lubkemann removes distractions to see what is plain and ordinary. He has clarity about hope and purpose, which allows him to do the extraordinary with an everyday knife and a pile of twigs.

Does simplicity lead to the discovery of hope and purpose? Can someone create a way of living that is unconventional, stick to it, and find joy as well as financial stability by living a simple life? In this interview, Chris Lubkemann reveals how the finding of a North Carolina mountain craft shaped his life and led to him to the discovery of hope and purpose.

ALBRECHT: You were born where?

LUBKEMANN: Brazil, in Sao Paulo City. My folks were in the interior. Who knows what hospital they had?

ALBRECHT: But you're not Brazilian?

LUBKEMANN: Well... the Brazilians would consider me Brazilian because if you are born in Brazil, you're a Brazilian, no matter what. In fact, my dad and mom were going to get expelled from Brazil because they were not Brazilian before World War II, but my dad said that we have a Brazilian son.

The Brazilians said, "You have a Brazilian son?"

"Born in Sao Paulo."

"Oh, you can stay." I was the reason they were allowed to stay because I was a Brazilian.

My parents were missionaries there, jungle missionaries. My mom was the first Caucasian woman in the world to enter certain parts of the Amazon back in the 40s. She was maybe thirty years old serving at one of the tributaries of the Amazon. They had a rubber boat for the rapids. Some of the tribes had never seen an outside woman—not too many men, or no men, either. She had light skin. That was a novelty. She wore something. That was a novelty. They didn't wear anything—a few feathers, and that was about it. When they went away, we stayed with one of the other missionary families. When they returned, you know how they signaled us? They lit a fire. As that fire just burned, it came toward us. That was probably 1948, or something like that.

I remember a few things from when I was four, but when we went to Peru from when I was six to nine, I can remember it like it was just yesterday. My dad—he was from New York City and worked in a hardware store. He knew a little bit about tools, and he had to build a lot of stuff. In Brazil, his work bench was under a mango tree. In any case, pieces of wood fell from his workbench, and I got down and made little toys. When I was eight, I had a little girlfriend. I made her a little highchair. But anyway, I do not like dentists, but for some reason I started carving dental tools—little picks, and we started playing in each other's mouths. My mother was from western Kansas, and she said, "Oh no, guys. No picking in other people's mouths." I think she thought us jungle kids would get some rare disease. So, she put the kibosh on my dental career. I was just six or seven.

We were in a really primitive situation there. The only way to get into the jungle part of Peru toward the beginning of the Amazon was either by seaplane, one of those beaver pontoon planes, or riverboat. The town had one street along that river. We went around barefoot—got parasites and worms. The worst thing I had to do is take bung gareena- the deworming mix. That's where I started working with wood, just as a six-, seven-, eight-, nine-year old kid.

The next thing I had with wood was a shop class in eighth grade at a boarding school. That was the only time I had formal training in wood. I don't remember what we did.

I never went back to Brazil after college at twenty-two because I would have been drafted into the Brazilian army just like that, and I just didn't want that. I had a student classification here in the States. I could have been right in the Brazilian Army, but I thought, nah, I don't want that. I might have liked the cavalry though. Back in our interior town, they had beautiful horses. In fact, I have not been back to Brazil since 1957.

I ended up going for four years to Columbia Bible College, which is now called Columbia International University. From year to year, I did not know what would be the next year, so I ended up taking senior courses my freshman year. I ended up taking freshman courses my junior and senior year. The freshman didn't appreciate them (the classes), but I did because I could see the value of them. But they started them out freshman year in world history or something like that. I had a fantastic teacher, a Princeton guy, and they didn't appreciate the course, but I did because I was a senior. I saw the usefulness of it. I had sort of a convoluted college career.

ALBRECHT: So, your senior year, you come to your senior year, and you're faced with a problem—money. What happened?

LUBKEMANN: I had a little bit of scholarship. There was this neat guy, a treasurer for a bunch of carpet companies in Georgia, Nel Keller, and he—ya know, we were missionary kids, we did not have a lot of money—he gave some scholarships, so I had a little bit of scholarship money from him, not much. So, I had to work, like many college students. I had the choice. The campus was four miles outside of the City of Columbia, so I would have to get some kind of transportation into Columbia. Going back and forth would take time and money.

So, I picked up this idea in the summer of 1966 in western North Carolina, right up in the corner near Tennessee and Virginia. And, I got this idea, and I thought I could make it work. In fact, I have it here right in my pocket. I found a knife, like one of the early ones that I bought for a $1.95. It was probably made by Imperial Knife Company in Providence, Rhode Island. It was a little different from this knife [referring to a Swiss Army knife he produced from his pocket]. But, when I went to college, I went to help this old minister with his youth program at these little mountain churches that had former moonshiners. This was back in the boonies, no paved roads going into some of these places. That's when I saw these little things carved from tree branches. I started that summer with Dr. Luke—John Luke—he was fantastic, and he was a minister there, and I said, "How in the world do you make one of these things?" [referring to a whittled rooster made from a twig] He could do anything. He was sixty-eight years old. I considered him old then. I was about twenty-one. He knew how to do it. He went out to his backyard or his side yard and got some twigs. You see, that was one of the main things they sold there in western North Carolina—things made out of twigs. These were the mountain people. And so, I took my Barlow knife and made my first one. It looked like it got into a horrible fight. So, I kept carving that summer.

When I went back to college my senior year, I said right away, I'm going to do this [whittling] to help pay for college because it took no travel time, and there were no transportation costs. I might have made more per hour at a conventional job, but in the long run and at the end of the year, I had netted the same amount I would have netted going into town after paying for all kinds of expenses, and I had a lot more fun doing it. I had a little toy wood burner, and I took that, and I began woodburning a little bit. The first thing I started doing is wood burning little pins, name pins. My fiancé at the time, my wife now, said, "Make one that says Cherie, and make one that says Chris." I thought, *I am not going to make my own name pin.* Can you imagine a guy walking around with his name on? So, she had me make a pin that said *Cherie – Chris.* It was a small campus, and it got to the point where every steady couple ordered a couple of name pins. Those were the main things—the roosters and the name pins. That ended up paying for school and a little bit of graduate school, and I took some special courses also different years. I had some bills to pay. I went into a restaurant that served chicken, and I offered to make name pins for the waitresses, the servers. So, their pin had a little rooster on a little log that had a name on it. That paid for some bills too.

It was kind of a hobby, but it just became a fun way to pay for bills—college bills, laundry and grocery, and fifty-three years later, I have never lost the fun of it. Everything is different. You never make two things exactly alike. Your branches are there, and I have come up with a lot of other ideas besides the rooster. I make Dr. Seuss-like characters. I will tell people about the story of a carving, like it is a real animal, and at the end they realize, oh, that never really happened.

- **2** -

WHEN I FIRST asked Chris Lubkemann if he was willing to be interviewed, I was after a raw story about a man who was resourceful. Chris has honed a unique skillset. If he picks up a willow branch, immediate words about what he sees will start dancing out of his mouth—a snake, a rooster, an owl, or one of his Dr. Seuss-like characters. The development of desire and unbridled vision are the first steps on the pathway to developing hope and purpose.

Running long distances hurts. I am big boned, have large, thick legs, and I sweat a lot. My daughter is built like a coat rack—sleek, tall and thin. She has long legs. Her ten-mile jogs end with talk and smile. After ten miles, I grunt. She looks like a jaguar with her hair sweat-slicked back. I look more like an old mule on a desperate search for a watering hole. However, after watching my daughter run all through high school and in college, I found that running is as much a sport as it is an art. A graceful runner is a thing of beauty, and within the running community, there is a positive vibe, comradery, and good mental and physical health. So, even though I am not built to be a distance runner, I run distances because the mental and physical health that I have found through running far outweighs the three knee surgeries and the stiffness that seem to be coming on with age. I followed in my daughter's footsteps, just at a much slower pace.

March 13th—Friday the 13th, 2020—is significant. Along with my routine of running, I teach. It is significant to note that three days prior to this date, I interviewed Chris Lubkemann. When I did the interview with Chris, I did not know that the looming COVID-19 virus was about to change the way people around the world conducted their daily habits and way of living. By that Friday, the library we met in was locked tight. No patrons were allowed. Almost overnight, a school superintendent's conference day that was supposed to be devoted to developing literacy skills and mental wellness was quickly transformed into a day of learning a foreign computer application called Microsoft Teams. We spent the day training so that *in the event* of a school closure, we would be teaching from a computer to maintain our students' skill level. Within days, this virus created a widespread panic that shifted the way I was about to teach. My level of technology competency is similar to the way I run—clunky. I can do it, but I am a turtle in the world of technology.

That Friday, we thought we would have school on Monday. Even on Sunday morning, school was still on. Within hours, all hell broke loose. By Sunday night, school was indefinitely cancelled, and we had two days to figure out how to start teaching remotely for an indefinite amount of time. Supermarket shelves were stripped. The two items at the local Walmart that sold out first were toilet paper and bullets. By Wednesday, with rubber gloves on, cars pulled up to the school in single file to be given their sanitized one-to-one laptop and all materials that each student would need to continue learning. With no end date in sight, we were giving out materials blind. By that Friday, the governor of New York began shutting down non-essential businesses, the stock market crashed, and kids discovered that they now had a new laptop toy. I quickly learned that a messaging chat between two fourth graders goes something like this: "Hi!" – emoji – "Hi!" – stupid emoji – "You're weird." – "an even stupider emoji." – etc.

Lines began forming at grocery stores at 5:00 AM for their 6:00 AM opening. New stock was quickly hoarded. The term social distancing, the antithesis of *Seinfeld's* close talker, was introduced. The news blitzed out information that whatever we touched or breathed on put our lives and families at risk. The virus was beginning to claim thousands of lives per day, and if we did not want to be a statistic, we had to self-isolate. Three weeks into the American standstill, I had a routine. I got up and answered emails from students and parents. At 9:00 AM I ate breakfast and took the dog for a walk. At 10:00 AM I went online to teach by video for three hours. The first week it was new; by week three, it was exhausting. My students' attention spans were waning too. At 1:00 PM, I ate lunch, and then I gave myself a break. I went for a lot of runs. I showered, created the next day's lessons, evaluated the current day's typed responses, and emailed families daily progress updates. Evening cocktails went up. I was stress drinking, and my life felt a lot like Bill Murray's nightmare in the movie *Groundhog Day*.

I live in the same town that I teach. Brockport, New York is a little farming suburb of Rochester. My home is about five miles south of Lake Ontario. The 200-year-old Erie Canal runs right through the heart of our village, and the original towpath that oxen used to pull boats from the Hudson River in Albany to Lake Erie in Buffalo still exists. The trail is covered with cinder stones and is soft on my aging legs. The canal path is perfect for an amateur jogger like me. It is peaceful, flat, and best of all, usually underused. In other words, I avoid embarrassment by running on the towpath because I see very few people in passing. It is one of the few places that I run shirtless on hot days.

As the days went on during the semi-quarantine, I got into a routine of running after lunch. I have jogged on the canal for nearly fifteen years. It has always been rare to see a lot of people walking or running even on the most beautiful days. However, as we went further and further into isolation, I noticed more and more traffic on the canal. On a ten-mile jog in March, which can be a chilly month, just a year before, I may have seen three to four passersby. By week three of the pandemic, I began counting people. Some days I would pass over one hundred and fifty people, mostly walking in small family groups, often with a dog. Ironically, during one of the unhealthiest times in modern history, people were making healthier decisions. Most individuals were making eye contact as I ran by, and a joyful hello was exchanged. Folks were longing for human contact.

During that time, people lost a lot—freedom of places to go, money, and jobs. Gathering spots like recreation centers, the YMCA, restaurants, and theaters were closed. All the unnecessary distractions of life were gone too. The elimination of so many things that prevent people from seeing the obvious were rapidly disappearing. Not only were people losing a lot of money, but there were also no places to spend it, if they had it in the first place. I went eight weeks without filling up my car with gas. Distractions were gone, and all that was left were the simple and obvious things that were right in front of people—coloring books, boardgames, and a beautiful canal path rich in history and complete with an occasional heron taking flight along its banks. The dreadful pandemic uncovered a silver lining by removing so much of the complexity of life. People had been so caught up in rushing that they forgot to stop and smell the roses; the concept that had become so foreign that people had nearly no sense of smell for lack of use. The canal that was neglected by many was being rediscovered. For a moment in time, the virus had stripped a lot of life's options and employment away, and what was left were family walks. The basic need for human interaction was rediscovered, and people were smiling and saying hello in passing.

I had the honor to spend a few days with Chris Lubkemann. His work of whittling, which he calls a hobby, has been his lifeblood and livelihood for over fifty-three years. Lubkemann grew up with little money. He was the son of missionaries and lived in remote areas of Peru and Brazil for the first nine years of his life. The distractions of modern America were not part of his upbringing; he had to make do with what he had, and so found himself under his father's workbench making objects out of wood scraps. Lubkemann's upbringing in a solitary place, a tributary to the Amazon, created an environment where he could see what was right in front of him and led to a life with few distractions.

Years later, a financially struggling Lubkemann would be taken to the mountains of western North Carolina. He would observe the twigs from trees, though they could have easily been overlooked, and watched whittlers whose craft had been honed in isolation and passed from generation to generation. He also discovered that the craft was not nearly as easy as it looked. If Lubkemann was going to be successful, he was going to have to devote himself to hard work, careful observation, and the willingness to learn from his failures. Every skill he needed to become a master whittler parallels what guides people to the discovery of hope and purpose. Lubkemann described the product of his first attempt at carving a rooster as one *that got into a bad fight.* However, with practice, he became a whittler, and used his newfound craft to pay his way through college with an inexpensive pocketknife and twigs. Even decades later, Lubkemann still radiated with joy when detailing his discovery of his path to hope.

The path to hope and purpose starts with an uphill run. The obvious little things that make us happy must be rediscovered. For this to happen, all the distractions that clutter the garage of life have be cleaned out. Disconnection cannot be temporary. It is easy to slip back into old habits, but hope is hard to achieve because it takes hard work—and that takes time. Hope is not recognized in an instant. Rubbing off a lottery ticket is a wish. Wishes are not part of the path of hope. There is little complexity in a career made from sticks and an inexpensive pocketknife, but a disciple of hope is born out of years of practice. Lubkemann is the author of five books about whittling, and his book written for Victorinox—the manufacturer of the Swiss Army knife—is the number one bestselling book in the world on whittling. The simplicity of his life allowed him to recognize hope and purpose, which guided him to contributing to the world.

In 1988, Yellowstone National Park faced the most devastating fires in United States history. A total of 250 separate fires—forty-two caused by lightning and nine started by humans—burned a total of 793,800 acres, or thirty-six percent of the park. An exceptionally dry summer, wind, and an overabundance of dense brush and dead trees all contributed to this historic disaster.

The fires lasted from the middle of June through mid-November and forced the complete closure of the park in September. At first, people thought the charred park would be permanently scarred and destroyed, but something unexpected happened. For most conifers, fire is an essential element of life. Fire causes pinecones to open and expose their seeds, and within years of the blaze, lodgepole saplings began to emerge from the ashes. Nature and people are similar. Both sometimes need a purging to encourage the possibility of hope emerging.

Noticing something that you never saw or considered—a smile, a walk, or even a twig— reminds us that the beginnings of hope and purpose are found right in front of us. Hope is never gained; it exists waiting to be recognized. Identifying what brings people hope is not enough. Like Chris Lubkemann, if hope is going to become habitual, a lot of work must be done to keep it fresh as part of our daily routines. In an increasingly demanding world, finding hope is one of the simplest and most difficult things that can be done.

- **3** -

THE FIRST WESTERN European explorers began coming to North America in the late 15th century. Many settlements failed as starvation, disease, and lack of skills in this uncharted land proved to be both challenging and fatal. The early colonists lacked the knowledge of how to survive in this new land. Growing food in this unfamiliar climate presented an additional challenge, and linguistic and cultural differences between groups meant that each settlement started from scratch. A huge part of the issue was the type of people who were going to the "New World." Born to middle- and upper-class sons who were too far down the line of succession to inherit anything, many of the settlers were people who did not know how to survive. They did not understand farming with crops and animals, sewing and mending, or even basic construction.

It took nearly 115 years of trial and error, from the landing of Columbus to the first permanent settlement in Jamestown, for colonists to learn how to survive in this new land. To put this into perspective, the Wright brothers got the first airplane to fly 800 feet before crashing in 1903. By 1917, war planes were flying over Europe, and within sixty-six years, Neil Armstrong became the first human to walk on the face of the moon. The shift from being earthbound to mastering space travel took half the time of western Europeans creating a successful settlement. Based on the range of time it took from exploration to colonization, survival in a new land was embracing a mindset of defying the impossible.

In most Native American nations in the Northeastern woodlands, three staples are celebrated as the Three Sisters: corn, beans, and squash. Natives planted seeds of the three together. Their relationship is quite practical. Corn grows a stiff and strong stalk, beans climb the stalk, and the broad leaves of the squash cover the ground, keeping precious moisture in the soil. I learned this while I was on a field trip at a museum dedicated to the Haudenosaunee (Iroquois). Ever the skeptic, I planted the seeds together, tended to them daily, and lo and behold, during a summer of drought, the crops grew healthy and strong.

What were the earliest colonists thinking about? What was

important to them, and did those priorities not allow them to see what was right in front of them? In the modern world, cell phones, television, compulsive buying, poverty, and a various assortment of distractions create a fog that keep people from seeing the obvious. The distractions are found across all socio-economic classes. Though they lived centuries ago, the colonists certainly had distractions of their own. After all, the Native Americans had clearly built successful societies; they had the answers that would allow the colonists to not only survive, but thrive. Instead of trying to fight the Native Americans, why not just ask for help? The colonists had the soil and seeds to succeed, but they could not figure out the miracle of the Three Sisters. What were on the minds of the early colonists? Alcohol, and lots of it!

Florida was being explored by the Spaniards by the mid-sixteenth century. European shelters were primitive, and healthcare was minimal, but by 1563 the first wine was being made by harvesting the abundance of grapes growing wild in this semi-tropical land. Like the distraction of a cell phone, the Spaniards were too busy making wine to worry about survival. Today, it seems like we cannot survive without a phone; a parallel addiction crippled the Spaniards. They were not alone. By 1587, the first beer was being brewed in the colonies in Virginia by Sir Walter Raleigh's colony. Corn was in abundance, so most beer was brewed from corn (or maize, as it was locally known).

Dr. William J. Rorabaugh is a professor of history at the University of Washington. He has studied alcohol consumption in the New England colonies; his numbers are based on the research of historian James E. Royce. When 132 Puritans boarded the Mayflower in 1620 for its voyage across the Atlantic Ocean, there was quite the collection of alcohol in their inventory. Wisely, they packed fourteen tons of fresh water to go along with the forty-two tons of beer. They brought 10,000 gallons of wine, too, ac-counting for approximately forty-five tons of the drink. Once they arrived in North America, early settlers made alcoholic beverages out of everything from cranberries to oak leaves. Historians A.D. Eames and Michael Prendergast show in their work that alcohol affected every aspect of colonial life, including insurance, meet-ing places, and even pregnancy!

In the context of what is classically taught about the early co-lonial settlements in North America, explorers and colonists rep-resent hope in a new land—and escaping the rules and tyranny of many European countries. Hope is discovered when the distrac-tions of wants are removed. Today, an argument could surely be made that cellphones, computers, and televisions have replaced books. The hyper-focus on finances, careers, and the demands of the workplace dominate peoples' lives. There is a natural sense in large populations to be critical and project negativity towards new thinking and creativity. All of this is unnecessary and creates a smokescreen that prevents people from seeing what is truly im-portant.

Alcohol consumed the minds and actions of the early colonists. Alcohol was a want, not a need. Its rampant use blocked colonists' ability to discover hope, so it took a full 115 years for the first per-manent European settlement to be established. There was hard-ship in colonial America, but the chronicles of the Wright broth-ers were full of accounts of mosquito infestations and challenging weather on desolate sand dunes. They got a plane to fly after only four years of experimentation, and the world was using the airplane as a weapon of war within fourteen. The people work-ing on the airplane discovered hope, though it is paradoxical to associate hope with the First World War. The use of the airplane as a tool of war demonstrates that advances were made quickly because few distractions diminished the need for a better weapon. Early colonists faced starvation, poor shelters, and a general lack of survival knowledge. Had they removed distractions like the heavy focus on alcohol and style, hope would have emerged at a much faster rate. When hope is present, success thrives. Distractions cause hope to wither like autumn foliage.

As a teacher, I believe that ignoring a child is one of the greatest forms of abuse. Children that are ignored tend to seek attention in any way possible. If a caregiver is so preoccupied with distractions, then they themselves have not found hope. Whatever the distraction—electronics, drugs, sleep, or compulsive spending, to name a few examples—blinders pop up that detract from the necessary work of raising a child. Being disregarded or unnoticed causes the child to feel a loss of purpose and, consequently, they feel worthless. The effects compound: apathy, lack of remorse, and a sterile sense of joy. A lot of ignored children, by nature, will seek attention in any way they can; if misbehavior gets them attention, they misbehave. As teens, promiscuity, taking dares, and other attention-seeking behaviors develop. These develop into distractions that repeat in a cancerous cycle when the next generation is born.

The answer to making progress towards a better tomorrow is within everyone's grasp: give children attention for doing positive behaviors. This develops the child's understanding of purpose, which builds hope. This is a time-consuming job that requires patience. Hope is a lifelong body of effort, and therefore breaking the habits of generations is difficult. A parent who only understands how their parent behaved must relearn an entirely new lifestyle. It is hard to fathom, so in real life, it is a very challenging barrier to overcome. However, excuses need to end, lines need to be drawn, discipline must be developed, and the moment a person becomes a parent, the parenting must be made priority number one.

The discovery of hope and purpose takes discipline. The removal of the shroud of distraction, constant effort, and ongoing plans are necessary to avoid disturbances. Is hope easy to maintain? Absolutely not. The discovery and maintenance of hope takes lifelong commitment. There is no end. It is not like earning a million dollars. Once a million dollars is earned, the threshold is met. Hope has no threshold and is like an ever-growing bush. It needs pruning, fertilization, and a lifetime of attention if it is going to be healthy. Even one year of neglect can have catastrophic consequences. Hope takes a lot of discipline and work; both are personal choices.

CHAPTER 2
ALL CHIPS IN

The Board of Trade shall deliver to every applicant who is duly reported by the examiners to have passed the examination satisfactorily, and to have given evidence of his sobriety, his experience, his ability, and his general good conduct on board ship, such a certificate of competency as the case requires.

-Canada Shipping Act, 1938

- 1 -

Living vicariously through my daughter's five years of high school running and four years as a collegiate long-distance runner, I have recognized that there is a clear gap between men's and women's sports, regardless of the Title IX legislation. Men's sports get greater advertising, more television time, and have more professional leagues. As a dad, I have made a deliberate effort to expose my daughter to female runners such as Wilma Rudolf, Joan Benoit Samuelson, and runners of her era like Jenny Simpson and Mary Cain with the goal that she would pick up on their mental strength and work ethic. These are women who are household names only in the homes of runners but live in obscurity, unlike many male athletes.

Prior to 1972, rules prohibited women from registering for the Boston Marathon. In 1972, Title IX laws were passed, which forced the country toward evening the playing field between men and women. Laws place boundaries on what rules people can impose, but they do not instantly change mindsets. This takes time, which can often outlive the lawmakers and those that broke ground in the first place.

Kathrine Switzer was the only woman on the Syracuse University cross country team. Her first name has been spelled wrong so many times (Katherine), that she often signs her name as K.V. Switzer. Self-described as bold and feisty, and encouraged by her coach, Arnie Briggs, K.V. Switzer made the decision to register for the Boston Marathon and went under the radar to receive bib number 261. It was 1967. Today, it seems almost unfathomable that gender would prevent a person from entering a running contest. In 1967, gender was a limiting factor.

Prior to 1972, the Boston Athletic Association would not allow female participants to register for the Boston Marathon. Somewhere around mile four, Switzer was attacked by a race official from the Boston Athletic Club, Jock Semple, for violating the gender-restrictive rules. He wanted the bib number back. Protected by her coach and her nationally recognized hammer-thrower boyfriend, on April 19, 1967, Katherine Switzer had to dig deep into her soul to finish the race. In doing so, she became the first registered female to run the Boston Marathon and became a living inspiration among women in sports. In 1980, the average field in a marathon was ten percent female. Today, nearly half of all marathon finishers in the United States are women.

Kathrine Switzer is a commentator for televised marathons and is the author of two books: <u>Running and Walking for Women Over 40</u> *and* <u>Marathon Woman,</u> *which won the Billie Award in journalism for its inspiring portrayal of women in sports. In 2011, Switzer was inducted into the National Women's Hall of Fame; in 2015, she launched a global non-profit organization called 261 Fearless, which focuses on using running to empower women to overcome life obstacles and embrace healthy living. What is the impact of diversity on the discovery of hope and purpose? Does*

*the understanding of the context of historical events create an
impression on the development of hope? Can one person's example have a direct effect on other people's abilities to develop hope
and purpose? Switzer's life experiences can speak to both.*

ALBRECHT: What's it like in New Zealand where you are?

SWITZER: Beautiful. This morning we woke up, and it looked like
a painting outside. We live on a- not quite a cliff but a very high
hill overlooking Wellington City, the harbor, and the mountains.
I'll send you a picture. It is absolutely gorgeous. This morning, the
whole basin, if you will, up to the mountain peaks on the other
side had a big white cloud. The mountains were just popping up
behind it with the sun popping up behind that. It was just amazing, just gorgeous. Anyway, it is just late summer- early autumn,
and the weather is just gorgeous. Up to now it has been just utterly fantastic. I'm just pissed off because I have a bad Achilles
tendon, so I can only run about six or seven minutes with a couple of minutes in between because I am trying to recover the
thing. This weather is just perfect for doing three or four hour
runs with the beautiful scenery. So, you have a daughter that runs
at the University of Vermont, correct?

ALBRECHT: Yes, she is in her final year. She has had a really good
experience up there. You know, I think I have enjoyed her final
years of running the most. I spent some time talking with Abby
Wambach (US professional soccer player) at a speaking engagement. We were both talking about being sideline parents, and
Abby said when she watches her kids play soccer, she always
stands at the corner of the soccer field away from people and
carries lollipops, so she doesn't say a lot. She reminded me that
if Autumn is running at that level and running that well, the best
thing that I can do is support her and make her feel good about

her accomplishments. No matter how hard I yell, it is just not going to help her any. She never needs to be reminded to run, lift, or work on her core. She just does it. And you know how it is, distance runners are like a little bonding force of hope.

SWITZER: Yeah, and it is a universal language too. You often don't need sometimes to articulate what you're saying, and everyone will understand. And, when you're running together, you're not all talking, but we're all thinking the same thing. It is very strange how that works. [Laughs] I can remember being with Arnie Briggs. We did these three or four runs, and sometimes, like twenty or thirty minutes had passed until we realized that we hadn't said anything, but then somebody would start talking, and they would know exactly what the other person was thinking, and it would have nothing to do with what we had been talking about before. You know, it is very strange how that happens.

ALBRECHT: I am identifying people who are bringing hope to the world. After reading your books and hearing about you, I decided you are a person I want to talk about hope with. My understanding is that you started out life in Germany. Is that correct?

SWITZER: Yes, but I don't remember any of it. I was born in Germany. The profound experience from Germany came afterwards and by the way I was raised. My dad was in the Army. One of his jobs was to relocate displaced persons of which there were millions, and so I grew up on the stories of their life in Germany. The war was a defining moment in my parents' lives, just like I thought 9/11 was a defining moment in mine and maybe, rather, it is this virus. I was there until I was three, three and a half or so.

ALBRECHT: Was your dad a veteran of World War II?

SWITZER: Yes, he was, very much so. He was a major, and he didn't see action, which frustrated him extremely because you know guys want to go in and fight. He was a highly motivating guy. He had a university degree. He was huge, attractive, and very athletic- strong, so they had him in training all the time. I can see why, and he was training troops like mad. His first assignment was to go to Germany, but it was actually after the war. It was in early or mid '46.

ALBRECHT: So, did you move around a lot as an Army kid?

SWITZER: Not as much as you would think. After Germany we came back and were based in Arlington, Virginia. While we were there, my dad went into the Korean War. It was a quite frightening time for all of us. We thought we would be moving. We were packing to go to Japan. That trip was canceled, and he finished his tour of duty in Korea. We were in Chicago for three or four years and then came back to Washington, DC. My dad went to the Pentagon and got more into intelligence, and after some time he retired.

ALBRECHT: Wow, that is quite a career.

SWITZER: So, I was mostly raised in the Washington, DC area. That is where I graduated from high school. I took my first years of college at Lynchburg College, in Lynchburg, Virginia, and then transferred to Syracuse so I could study journalism.

ALBRECHT: Good school for journalism.

SWITZER: Yeah, that's why I went.

ALBRECHT: You are seventy-three now. You have led an active life. Thinking about yourself now, how would you describe yourself?

Switzer: Oh gee, I would describe myself as, um, an older, feisty, very fit woman who still believes that one person can do a lot to change the world. I have hope that this is true, but I despair like other people of the vicissitudes of politics, and I despair but have hope of humans disdain they have for the environment. And, I have hope and belief that in my lifetime we will see a real and true emergence of strong and empowered women. I really haven't thought about that. I was trying to say it in as few words as possible.

ALBRECHT: I think you said a lot. One of the big concerns—I spoke at a college in 2018, the hundredth anniversary of women's suffrage in New York State, and of course we are now in 2020, the hundredth anniversary of women gaining the right to vote nationally. As a fourth-grade teacher it blows my mind so little talk or curriculum has come about it. I am making sure it is covered. I talk to my daughter about that all the time, keep that fight going, because if you don't keep your ground, and hold your ground, you lose ground.

SWITZER: You know that I just wrote what you said down in red ink—no curriculum for women's suffrage. I find that, particularly in upstate New York, appalling. Education is everything, just everything. When I grew up and went to high school, I didn't even know who Susan B. Anthony was. It wasn't even brought up, so this was all stuff I practically had to learn while I was I college. It's amazing. When we talk about the right to vote to a kid, they think it was a million years ago, but let me tell you the most amazing story...

When I ran the Boston Marathon in 1967, people even now say to me, even young women, even teenage girls, they say that wasn't even that long ago what that guy tried to do to you, pull you out of the race. Well, the distance in years from 1920 to 1967 and 1967 to now, suffrage was a lot closer. Do you see what I mean? Why would you say that 1967 was not all that long ago when 1920 was not all that long ago? 1920 was not that long ago! I think that being our modern history, at least is talking about Vietnam, World War II, etc. like it wasn't that long ago, and with women's running, it is so much a big part of their lives, like your daughter. They can't imagine their lives without running. And so they are astonished that this amazing feeling and transformational experience for them is relatively new in historic terms.

I have sixty and seventy-year-old women who come up to me who have only started running, and they are like kids. They say things like *oh my God, I was never an athlete. I was never allowed to be an athlete. Now I am. My kids are grown up. I can do what I want. I'm traveling the world. I'm going to Tokyo next week- that kind of thing.* It has opened this whole world to them, and they say, *I always thought that there was always a women's marathon in the Olympic games.* They just don't know about the discrimination in their own lives. It is amazing.

ALBRECHT: Going back two years, I spoke at a local college to a group of women who support females with scholarships. I talked about the year, 1918. So few people, even the older ladies, knew that it was the 100th anniversary of suffrage in New York State.

SWITZER: Oh, wow.

ALBRECHT: I talked about that. This was a real good wakeup call because we need to remember our history. When we forget our history, we make the same mistakes twice.

SWITZER: I made a speech in Rochester a year and a half ago. It was kind of a dual thing. I was a speaker, then I had the afternoon afterwards. I had a whole next morning, and Rochester women had me come run with them, and I did. They asked, "Where would you like to run?" I told them that I would like to see a little of Rochester, because I had driven through it a million times, but I had never seen it. I had no idea, that it was a hotbed for really, for- really the whole area felt like a utopian kind of colony. I had no idea that Susan B. Anthony had actually *lived* there. Frederick Douglass- I love the statue of the two of them having tea in that small park. I went to the house. I had no idea that this stuff existed here. This is amazing, absolutely amazing.

ALBRECHT: What I love about Susan B. Anthony's house is they haven't gussied it all up. They have left it in the same style from when she lived in it. She really wasn't a wealthy woman. You think of her and think that she must have had some money. She didn't. She put it all toward her cause. She was all chips in.

SWITZER: Well, I know that feeling. People come to visit me and they kind of look around and say, "She lives modestly."

ALBRECHT: Do you live modestly?

SWITZER: I do. I have what you would call an extravagant lifestyle if you consider that I live in two countries. It is enormously expensive to fly back and forth. That is why I only do it twice per year. We bought very cheap houses and every year do a little something. I would say that I have pretty much given away a lot of my money to the 261 Foundation. You create a nonprofit, it costs a lot of money- lawyers, accountants, all that stuff.

ALBRECHT: You are in a tremendous position to help other people, so I see it as the right thing to do.

SWITZER: Yeah, I think so. Money doesn't interest me, but what it does interests me. When I look at—I have got to read her book, Melinda Gates's book, their spending billions trying to fix things in the world, and because of different administrations, it somehow manages to disappear. So, you have to be on top of it, but what money can do, if correctly placed, is quite phenomenal. Sometimes, it's not a lot of money. That's why my foundation is about running—it is cheap, easy, and accessible, and it changes your life. It doesn't cost anything, and when you have a group of women or a group of girls, it is very uplifting, empowering, a sense of friendship, but you have to make sure that it is non-judgmental, especially with young girls. They can be kind of crappy to each other sometimes. We got to get them beyond that.

There is a company that I work with in New Zealand—I can talk to you about this because you are a teacher and because of your daughter. They created this menstrual cup. And this is fantastic for women athletes. In fact, I would love to send one to your daughter. And you get through a marathon—you can't run a marathon when you're in your period very well. I always wore black tights. We can laugh about it here because we have sanitary protection, but if you go to Africa, and the girls don't. They're poor. So, they miss a week of school every month. They stay home, they sit on their grass mat and feel ashamed, dirty, and excluded because everyone knows that they are home bleeding. At the end of the year, they have missed two months of school, and ya know what, by the time they are sixteen or seventeen, they are never going to catch up in their education, so they drop out, and it is an endless cycle. If you simply can break that cycle by giving them a product that they can use that is cheap and can be used again and again—the lifespan of this thing is eight years. It is totally hygienic, but you have to give them lessons on how to use it, how to keep it clean, all that kind of stuff. And that's cheap in terms of an educational program. So, what I am saying is that I am interested in money when it can be well-placed, administered, and make a difference. These are things that give me hope. A few conscientious people working conscientiously together can make a huge difference. That is what we are doing at my foundation, and that gives me a lot of hope.

ALBRECHT: Kids are thirsty for hope. Kids want to talk about these issues, sometimes more than adults do, but they do not have a lot of vision, and it is talked about less and less. As a teacher, I observe that, and I realize that is a place where I have to put some caulk within in the bricks of the wall of learning.

SWITZER: Yeah, that's good. You know, I am a real Pollyanna [a character who believed that most problems could be solved with a positive attitude] about this virus [COVID-19], but now I think there is a whole wave of people saying *holy shit, you know, I really never really had time for my kids because we were all so busy. Now I really have this opportunity to be with them and talk to them.* I really, really have a lot of hope with this because the cellphone and the internet—maybe we don't have to just be a slave to that. Maybe, we can once again, sit around the dining room table or the fireplace, talk about things and get to know each other. I am really hopeful with that.

ALBRECHT: Who is your favorite teacher? If you could pick just one person who was influential, an amazing teacher, who would you pick?

SWITZER: There would be two. The first is—believe it or not, my mother was my fourth-grade teacher. We lived outside of Chicago in a growing suburb. She had a teaching certificate. They really needed teachers. I was old enough to be home alone, so she decided to take the teaching job, and I was in the fourth grade. She had forty students! I was taught like everyone else. There was no favoritism, no recognition that she was my mom. When I raised my hand, I addressed her as Mom, not Mrs. Switzer, but that was it. I watched her style, and I could see why she was everybody's favorite teacher. She made everything a challenge, a contest, and fun. There was rote learning, but it was always fun.

The other teacher I had was my sixth-grade teacher. I was struggling with writing, believe it or not, and she realized that it was because I was left-handed, and she made me learn to write again. It was torture for me. She made me turn the paper the other way. She made me hold the pen, and she made me practice what was called in those days the Palmer Method. She had exquisite penmanship. She made extra money writing out wedding invitations to people. She also was a fantastic teacher. Boy, it was kind of like I couldn't wait for school, and normally, I hated school. I learned to write again.

ALBRECHT: And, then you went on to journalism school! What was your sixth-grade teacher's name?

SWITZER: Anne Carr—Dunn Loring Elementary School. She was hilarious! She always signed Christmas cards, and I got a Christmas card from her until I was about fifteen years old. It was really amazing. She must have had thousands of students in her lifetime, and she always signed her name *Anne Carr and how.* [lots of laughter]

ALBRECHT: If you had to pick three adjectives to describe your mom, what would they be?

Switzer: First would be fearless—utterly fearless. Bumps in the night, spiders, nope. Kind—extremely kind. And, the third is persistent.

ALBRECHT: And, how about Mrs. Carr?

SWITZER: Feisty, determined, demanding.

ALBRECHT: You described your mom as fearless. That is a name that is synonymous with you. Is that where *fearless* comes from, your mom?

SWITZER: No, it doesn't, but when I was describing my book, I tried to describe her. I realized that she went through a whole lot of deprivation, and my dad was also at war and overseas a lot. When she—well, the opening of my book is she got a doctor to lie about her pregnancy, so she could visit my dad to go live with him in Germany. She was on the first boat of dependents that left the United States to go to Germany. Her parents were furious with her. They said, "You have a little boy, and you are eight months pregnant. You are out of your mind. You can't do this." She got into the car, drove to New Jersey and left the car with my uncle. My uncle took her to the docks, she got on that boat, and it broke down in the North Atlantic. No lights, tossing back and forth—I was almost born in the North Atlantic. Can you imagine? No lights, being tossed back and forth in the North Atlantic, and she said, "Nope."

Fearless itself, the word, fearless, came in this really amazing way, organically. People began writing to me about five or six years ago saying that my bib number, 261, from the Boston Marathon made them feel fearless. They too, were told that they couldn't run or weren't worthy, and they began running, and they began feeling fearless, so they related to my story, and they related to 261. They would send me a picture, saying that tomorrow they were running in their first race and here is my bib number, but on my back I'm wearing 261, or I have it inked on my arm or here it is on my wrist. Then they started sending me pictures of their tattoos. When people tattoo your bib number, now that was really weird for me, and I got to thinking about it—they all used the word *fearless*. I thought we could speak and do something with it. We gotta do something with it sometimes. I didn't want to do a business. I just couldn't bear to do it; I couldn't bear to start another revolution. I kept saying to my team, "I'm too old for another revolution." We gotta do it, we gotta do it... so we created the foundation, the nonprofit, and it is going great. We are in eleven countries. I keep thinking *I've got to retire, please.*
Albrecht: You do not sound like the type that could ever stay retired.

- **2** -

THERE IS A small room above the garage that is the quietest place in my house. Two turtles share the room with me, and they always seem excited when I work up there. Their shells clonk against the tank a lot when I am in the room, and they will follow my finger back and forth as I swipe the tank. Like people, animals crave attention and stimulation. On the other side of their aquarium is a window that looks down the driveway and out to the street. My writing desk faces the opposite direction, looking out over our backyard and the woods. Sometimes I leave the writing desk and type in front of the turtle cage. For me, the presence of animals stimulates a part of my mind that can sometimes remain untapped.

On an early Sunday morning, I was typing in front of the turtle tank when a truck went racing through our neighborhood. The company name, Amazon, was on its side. Twenty minutes later another Amazon truck came through, then another, and over the course of the next three hours, five Amazon trucks made their way at varying speeds down our street to make deliveries on a Sunday morning. No doubt, Amazon believes in a seven-day work week.

I have bought products on Amazon. It is convenient, but the trucks racing through our neighborhood also remind me of a Venus flytrap. Nearly everything for sale on Amazon is brand new, which means over a three-hour time period, five deliveries of brand-new things came into my neighborhood, and they were coming in when I least expected them to be—on a Sunday morning. There really are few things that we need to survive that cost money. When it comes down to it, food and shelter are pretty much the only purchased goods that are necessary. However, even food can be grown. When I was young, I remember witnessing the less practiced art of canning and jarring food in my grandmother's kitchen. MomMom and PopPop's grocery bill was minimal because they grew a lot of their own food. Stories from my mother reveal that they ate a lot of chicken growing up because they raised them in the backyard and slaughtered them by hand. Amazon deliveries and supermarkets have us paying for the luxury of not having to grow and slaughter our food. We offset hard work through payments. Why would people jar food in the first place when it takes so much work? Hard work produces a product, and there is pride in that; pride allows us to cultivate a sense of self-belief, which in turn promotes the development of hope. How much work did it take to click and pay for those Amazon trucks?

I am not sure why, but before I spoke with Kathrine Switzer, I pictured a person living a complex life full of wealth. She lived in the spotlight, at least for a short time, and she travels the world speaking. Doesn't money equal an extravagant lifestyle? If she lived in my neighborhood, would one of those Amazon trucks have stopped at her house? She has a foundation, is a public speaker, and is a pioneer of women's global distance running. This interview busted those assumptions; Switzer came right out and said she prefers a life of modesty.

One thing that cannot be captured from her interview is the number of times she laughed, giggled, or expressed excitement in her inflection. The way a person speaks, not necessarily the words they choose, show their conviction, sincerity, and radiant hope. When Kathrine opened up about how people are surprised at her modest living style, she laughed a lot. She valued the view in New Zealand over having a fancy home, and if she had wheelbarrows of money, she would not have mentioned how expensive travel is from New York to New Zealand.

Likewise, her frustration with her healing Achilles tendon and her admission that money does not interest her show that Switzer's world is concerned with what is right in front of her—not clouded by Amazon trucks and fast purchases. I believe that is why Switzer is a runner. It is possible to run barefoot, so runners need almost nothing to pursue their sport. But long runs take time and a unique mindset; if a person's mind is distracted or cluttered with material goods, will they be able to go on a two-, three-, or even four-hour run? If they are in shape, yes, but will a runner sustain a lifestyle of running day after day if their life is cluttered? I do not believe so.

The world's population will exceed eight billion people over the next decade. Is it really possible for just one person to change the world? Absolutely. Jeff Bezos grew up poor, saw a huge opportunity in online retail, and had five Amazon trucks on my street on a Sunday morning. I live in only one of the millions of American neighborhoods those trucks are buzzing through. Did his ideas change purchasing habits? For sure. Whether the change he caused is a positive or negative one is an argument for a different book.

2020—when I am writing this book—is the 100th anniversary of women's suffrage in the United States. Much of the foundational work to achieve equality was laid down right where I currently live in Rochester, New York. When the nineteenth amendment to the Constitution was ratified, all politicians were male. If any group of people should be the poster citizens for hope, it would most definitely be the women of the suffrage movement. Consider the challenge they had to overcome. Not only were they erasing hundreds of years of traditional male-dominated leadership and decision making, but they also had to convince men to reverse it.

Fifteen states and territories, almost exclusively in the west, had granted women's suffrage prior to the ratification of the nineteenth amendment. After the first ten amendments contained in the Bill of Rights were agreed upon, there have only been seventeen other changes to the Constitution since 1791. An amendment is rare. Why is the 100th anniversary of suffrage not in the forefront of people's minds? Like Switzer, I have visited and toured the home of Susan B. Anthony. If there was not a sign out front, the house would blend into the urban neighborhood it sits in. It is not opulent or ornate. It is a simple home with few items that indicate that Susan B. Anthony collected little and was not distracted. Our docent told us that most of the money Susan B. Anthony had went to her cause.

Just one year prior to the centennial of the nineteenth amendment, 2019 marked the fiftieth anniversary of NASA's Apollo 11 mission, which landed the first people on the surface of the moon. It was all over the news and highly anticipated. As a teacher, I received frequent emails on STEM curriculum that promoted the moon landing. President Trump spoke about it frequently and tied it to his vision of putting the first person on Mars. I doubt when that day comes, people will look back on President Trump's drive to go to Mars like President Kennedy's challenge to go to the moon. Why? The answer lies in hope. Kennedy and the country were not clouded by self-gain when he made that challenge in Rice Stadium in Houston, Texas on September 12th, 1962. We had been challenged by the Soviet Union. The Soviets had put the first satellites and the first human into space. The country had a vision that included *purpose*. The anniversary of the moon landing was anticipated without hope, and now, less than one year later, we are not talking about it. The exploitation of historical events for political gain do not sustain or endure conviction.

Why then is the 100th anniversary of the passage of the nineteenth amendment not even making it onto the back pages of newspapers? Not all people with hope make it into the news. Couple this with the fact that it is very hard to imagine women not being allowed to vote. Few people have the good fortune to live to be 100 years old, and memories do not really start forming until late childhood. There are still many people left in the United States that know firsthand what it is like to not have the right to vote. Asian Americans were not allowed to vote until 1943, and Native Americans were unable to vote until 1965. Prior to 1964, many African Americans were prevented from voting via literacy tests, voting taxes, and other Jim Crow laws. As such, there is a large population of people who remember exactly what it was like to not be able to vote. Switzer made a point to note that her running in the Boston Marathon is closer in years to 1920 than 2020.

The passing of the nineteenth amendment is still young. Even younger are voting rights for female minorities. Many female athletes can remember a time where they did not see themselves in the same light as their male counterparts. Can one person change the world? Kathrine Switzer is proof that one person does make a difference. She is providing women with hope and purpose. Switzer has first-time runners in their sixties and seventies that never saw themselves as athletes or were never afforded the opportunity, suddenly discovering running. She stated, *I have hope and belief that in my lifetime we will see a real and true emergence of strong and empowered women.*

Belief causes vision. The liberation of a person's mindset has very few channels. Providing a person with hope and purpose is essential work that needs to be practiced daily if true liberation is to happen. This change does not take a lot of money, multiple Amazon trucks, or equipment. A person's mindset, in a sustainable situation, lives longer when it is not cluttered with distractions.

Switzer specifically pointed out that there are some essential components for hope and purpose to bloom; for their development in running to be uplifting, empowering, and stimulating, all people must remain nonjudgmental. Our world is inundated with ideals of what is considered a sexy body shape and stylish clothing. There is age discrimination and a separation of those with superior physical and mental abilities. The constant bombardment of these norms through social media, advertising, and a vast array of gimmicks has raised barriers that prevent people from hoping and having purpose. *I am overweight and embarrassed. If I run, I will not look like everybody else, so why try?* Switzer hit a bullseye when she emphasized that a core principle of her foundation is inclusivity, in an attempt to break down the shame and embarrassment that comes with feeling like you don't fit in. By doing so, she is allowing the girls she hopes to reach one less barrier to their rediscovery—or possibly their first discovery—of hope and purpose.

Switzer's admiration and love for her mother was clear. She was raised by two strong parents that instilled confidence in her through their example. Many parents take time to explain how to act, but do their actions parallel their words? The actions of one person have a much greater impact than the words of any speech. The enlightenment of Switzer's education comes through her fondness for her sixth-grade teacher, Anne Carr. Kathrine Switzer is left-handed and had reached the age of twelve before a teacher addressed her penmanship. This was an agonizing transition to relearn how to write, but it was necessary. Ms. Carr is described as a loving person. She sustained relationships with her students long after they left her class. No doubt Switzer admired this teacher because her current beliefs align exactly with Ms. Carr's teaching.

- 3 -

ALMA, NEW BRUNSWICK, Canada is situated to the west of Nova Scotia, across the Bay of Fundy. It was only a speck on the map until it was incorporated in 1966. Even today, the town only has a little over 200 residents. The Parish of Alma was developed in 1855 because of the Crimean War. Like many of the small settlements along the Bay of Fundy, people lived together to harvest the natural resources and transport them by ship. There is a near endless supply of lumber and stone, and the Bay of Fundy was and still is well protected from the elements to provide safe delivery of these much-needed resources to a growing population to the south. Though Alma remains small, its economy has shifted. The development of Fundy National Park increased tourism. The family-owned small business boats that supplied materials at the turn of the century have become more centralized, so people today make their living in the traditional ways of a century ago. The popularity of fishing has kept the boats in Alma. It remains a challenging place to live; blackflies and mosquitos are thick up though mid-July, and dense fog is common due to the warm and cold water mixing in the bay. The Bay of Fundy is also home to some of the highest tides in the world, sometimes reaching as great as twenty-nine feet.

Molly Kool was born into a man's world in Alma on February 23, 1916. Her solid relationship with her father was a major source of hope and purpose. At the time, less than two percent of people working on boats were girls or women. In nearly all cases, a woman working at sea was given laundry or cooking duties. There were also strict dress codes for women. They had to wear a dress that hung within ten inches of their ankles and had to wear long sleeves even on the hottest days. Through the fog, tides, and rough sailing conditions, Molly not only sailed with her father, but also played an important role on his ship.

Whether it was through superstition or pure sexism, at the time of Molly's birth, it was rare worldwide to see a woman anywhere near a boat. In Sweden, it was considered a bad omen if a woman asked a sailor where he was headed. In Quebec, if a fisherman saw a woman on his way to his vessel, it was a common practice for the man to turn around, head home, bless himself with holy water, and say a Hail Mary. British women could not step over a fishing line because it was believed this would cause a disaster at sea. As Molly Kool would put it when she was interviewed in 1939: "It was a belief that women were incompetent in a man's world and could not be trusted to learn seafaring skills." Ironically, boats are always referred to as *she*. Whatever the reason, Molly Kool worked with her father and most likely rarely saw another female.

As Kool sailed and worked with her father on the Bay of Fundy, she hoisted sails, ran and repaired the engines, sewed the canvas sails, navigated, and anchored the boats. She could steer a boat through rough waters and understood how to sail across tides. Kool was sent away from the galley because her attempts at cooking were a catastrophe. Kool and her father had a mutual respect, and his solid work ethic rubbed off on her. Before Kool finished her education, she had many months of experience on the sea. At school, she faced an education which encouraged girls to look pretty to attract the attention of males, while hiding any intelligences they had. In her heart, Kool did not fit in this world. Faced with her life in Alma, Kool really had two choices: conform or confront. Conformity is like a sledgehammer to the human spirit. When a person gives in—when society's expectation conflicts with a person's dreams—letting go of dreams causes a loss of hope, identity, and purpose.

Things in New Brunswick were changing slowly. Women gained the right to vote after years of failed attempts, but in 1928 the Supreme Court of Canada ruled that women, children, and the insane could not run for a seat on the Canadian Senate. It would not be until the following year that five women would challenge this law and gain the right to run for office. Pressures like these made Molly Kool consider pursuing a nursing degree after high school. Many women did. However, working at sea was not just something she was good at; it was something that made her happy. Working full-time for her father, she sharpened her skills passing through the Saint John River to deliver lumber and gravel. The Saint John River was laden with sandbars, and only the most experienced navigators were trusted at the helm. Kool's father let her sail there.

Kool's purpose in life was clear to her. After high school, she wanted to become a boat captain. No woman had ever been granted this title, though Kool had greater skills and experience than most males. She saw her purpose during a most unfortunate time. Throughout the Great Depression, unemployment in eastern Canada reached nearly 30%. Jobs were scarce, and it was the practice of the Canadian government to deter women from working, so men could be employed. A poster issued by the Canadian government in the mid-30s read: *Do you feel justified holding a job, which could be filled by a man who has not only himself to support, but a wife and family as well?*

Molly Kool was a teenager of the Depression. Her home lacked electricity or running water. Her income was vital to her family's survival, and her father needed a seaman. She did not take another man's job; she created an opportunity for her family even if it was not looked upon as the *correct* thing to do. Her belief in her mission and unwavering pursuit of her purpose makes her a masterful example of hope.

Being a working woman in the Bay of Fundy was one thing, but Kool hoped for more. She wanted to be a certified captain. Her father's health was in decline, and her skills were unquestionable. She was as seaworthy as any male, perhaps even more so. However, here is how the laws of the sea were written in the Canada Shipping act as of 1938: *The Board of Trade shall deliver to every applicant who is duly reported by the examiners to have passed the examination satisfactorily, and to have given evidence of his sobriety, his experience, his ability, and his general good conduct on board ship, such a certificate of competency as the case requires.* Every pronoun refers to only one gender—male. Kool was a woman. There was no changing that fact.

Early on when ships first sailed on the Bay of Fundy, a mariner did not need to be licensed. But as the commercial boat trade and industry began to grow, licensure was required. To achieve her goal, Kool aimed to be a certified mate. She studied in the city of Saint John when winter weather forced her boat to be docked there for an extended time. Her goal was not to be a ship's mate, but she believed that her experience and this certificate would allow her to attend mariner school. She would pass her mate exams with distinction. Immediately, she put in for her application to the Marine Institute in Yarmouth. No woman had ever applied there, and she was denied entry. She failed to give up and applied again—only to be refused a second time. If the institute would not bend, the pronouns in the law would be her only chance.

Kool took her case not to court, but to the media. She rallied pressure and never lost sight of her purpose. In 1939, under public scrutiny, the wording of the Canadian Shipping Act was changed. When it came time to be examined, Kool was tested in a separate room from the males. The school felt that having a woman present during exams would distract the males and lower their test scores. Laws do not necessarily change people's mindset. In 1939, after scoring a perfect grade at the age of twenty-three, Molly Kool became the first licensed female mariner in Canadian history.

It is easy to make a case that Kool led a liberation of gender bias, though she played down the changes in the laws. She simply wanted to be the captain of a ship. She was not after fame or a women's movement; she was living her life of hope and purpose. Kool stood as a testament that hope and purpose belong to the individual. She never lost sight of that.

I grew up playing baseball. In the 1970s, the garbage company in my hometown had a massive landfill that was completely full of decades of rubbish, so they put about eight feet of dirt over the dump and created a little league baseball complex. Back then, the fields were a maze of wire fencing and metal benches that turned white baseball pants gray in the butt if a player squirmed too much. There was a concession stand where the teams were printed on a wooden panel. Each team was sponsored by a business in town. I played for the local carpet store. The original Walter Matthau version of the Bad News Bears was not too far from reality. There was no such thing as a girls' softball league, so a lot of teams had one or two girls. Years later, the attending nurse at the birth of my son, Kristen, was not only a high school classmate, but also by far the best shortstop in the league.

My high school valued winning and coupled it with town pride. I pitched but I had a problem. I got to the point that I would throw up before games. There were no dugouts, just fencing, so puking was hard to hide. I would warmup deep in the outfield. There were trees that bordered a neighborhood. I routinely threw up before a start.

My senior year, I threw up in front of the assistant coach before throwing a two-hitter. The next day, the coach joined me on a long run, which was a common practice the day after a start. I was nervous and way too jacked up before starts. He gave me a piece of advice that I will never forget: *Nerves mean you care. Worry more about the day that you are not nervous.* It has stuck with me for thirty years, and I know it is true. When people get nervous it means they are either unprepared or they are truly invested in success. Growing up in a large town and making it onto a team of only sixteen players meant I had to work at throwing a baseball year round. I was more than prepared. I was nervous because I wanted to carry on a successful tradition. There was a loyalty to my team, my school, and myself. It was a life lesson.

Surely Switzer and Kool both had moments of doubt and nervousness. It is unavoidable when confronted with an obstacle to your aspirations. The moment people give up caring, and perhaps lose that knot of nervousness, one of two things happen. Either hope and purpose have been discovered, or they have disappeared altogether. When this time comes, it is important to realize that true growth occurs when a person is in discomfort and faces a reality. Living comfortably equates to standing still, which is a dangerous place to be. Only through progress or failure can things be learned. Progress happens when there is movement in a given direction—even the wrong one.

Throwing up may be a little over the top, but nerves, if channeled correctly, are an asset. Nerves coupled with effort and directed with precision always give a person a great chance of discovering and creating a life filled with hope and purpose.

Chapter 3
Purpose in Poverty

"I can—I will—No excuses. I am a gift to the world."
-Michael Warneke, Field of Dreams, Uganda

- 1 -

Michael Warneke is the founder and executive director of Field of Dreams, Inc. The mission of this non-profit organization is to "provide hope, empowerment and a future to the orphaned and vulnerable children of Uganda through the vehicles of soccer and education." Warneke oversees the organization, the Ugandan staff, and the United States volunteers. He is the lead advocate for raising funds and awareness for Field of Dreams with partner schools and orphanages. With an unequivocal charge, Warneke believes that it is a child's right to have avenues that allow them to reach their full potential as compassionate human beings, and it is the responsibility of all people to make sure that this happens. Warneke and his staff believe that the best way to do this is through education, particularly through their soccer programs and girl empowerment initiatives.

Warneke has a lot of experience working on-site with those he serves. Traveling from the United States to Uganda is expensive. How does bearing witness to those that are served increase the progress that is made? Time and money are the chief resources that affect the discovery of hope and purpose, right? Are there other factors that play a vital role that may not be as obvious or explicit? What role does practicality have when seeking to overcome the obstacle of inequity? Warneke's experience working with the people of Uganda to improve their lives sheds light on these questions and the path to hope and purpose.

ALBRECHT: It is great to have this time to talk with you.

WARNEKE: Well, I left Uganda on the ninth of March and got home on the tenth, and then the world turned upside down. Travel felt normal, but a week later, there are a lot of people in panic [over the COVID-19 virus]. It really felt like normal travel. It did not feel strange at all. They asked a few extra questions in the airport, and that was really it. Kinda shocked. As an organization, sustainability is one of our core values, and now, I keep telling our national director, "Johnathan, one day these borders are going to close." I always thought it was going to be for political reasons, but here we find ourselves, and I can't access our staff. Who knows when I will be able to get back there? It is just a strange time, for sure.

ALBRECHT: Well, I have followed your organization from its inception. Would you explain the function of your organization and its mission?

WARNEKE: It has been a journey for sure. One of the taglines of our organization is *hope is a basic need.* That's what we talk about in Uganda, and it is kind of at the forefront of what we do, even more so than get education and food, and all of those typical basic needs. If our kids lack hope, then there is nothing to look forward to. If you can't believe that tomorrow can be better than today, then we have given up. And so, we try to marry hope and purpose. I think that they are intertwined completely in Uganda, and so if we can teach these kids that they have purpose, then often hope is very quick to follow in their footsteps. So, I would even—I've seen it played out child, after child, after child—teacher, after teacher, after teacher, after teacher—and adult, after adult in Uganda. You can just see a physical change in these kids when they finally believe that tomorrow has some potential in it.

ALBRECHT: I am seeing the exact same thing as a teacher here in the United States. A lot of decisions point to poverty being the ultimate obstacle, but I tend to think that lack of hope is the greatest thing holding us back. A lot can be made out of nearly nothing, and hope is free. However, hope is something a person has to work for. Would you agree?

WARNEKE: You know, right now we have this virus thing here, but in Uganda, our kids are going to starve first before they ever deal with this virus, and it's because so many developing countries are locking down things. There is no way to get aid to our kids right now. Public transportation, private transportation, is all shut down right now, so to keep hope in the midst of that is a challenge—we are asking how our staff can continue to encourage through phone calls and texts just to ensure that our kids are not losing that piece.

ALBRECHT: How long have you been involved with Field of Dreams, Uganda?

WARNEKE: So, I went to Uganda—my first trip was eleven years ago, and it started—well, I am the founder of Field of Dreams, Uganda. We started putting the framework together nine years ago, and eight years ago is when we became a nonprofit. We had our first event in Uganda, a soccer tournament, on June 16th, 2012. It is the day of the African Child.

ALBRECHT: Let's go back to 2009. How did this all come to fruition?

WARNEKE: Well, at the time I had been—I was doing youth ministry in Quincy, Illinois. I was Director of Ministries at First Union Congregational Church, this tiny little church in Quincy, and I was doing thirty-hour famines. World Vision put on this deal—it was a lock-in where kids fast, and I found this group called Invisible Children out of Southern California. They made this film called *Invisible Children*, kind of uncut. I used that heavily with our youth group, especially during those thirty-hour famines. We would focus on Uganda, and kind of try to step in the shoes and lives of these kids. God just really broke my heart for Uganda. At that time, this would have been the mid-2000s. The Lord's Resistance Army was still really active in northern Uganda, so God just broke my heart for Uganda. I met this organization called Sweet Sleep twelve years ago. They said that the following year they were going to take their maiden voyage to Uganda. They had been working in Moldova, prior to that, and my wife Abby, who is just incredible, said that you need to do this. My son, Abel, was just a month old, and I got on a plane and headed to Uganda in July of the following year. That's kind of where my journey began. That first time in country there were twenty-three or twenty-four volunteers—didn't get to know the volunteers very well, they all knew each other, most were from around the national area. I kind of felt like a loner coming from Illinois. I just fell in love with the culture and the people.

We went to two orphanage schools that first trip. One was called Africa Greater Life, which was one of our founding partner schools, and the other was called Caring Heart Orphanage. We kind of split days for about eight or nine days. Two things struck me more than anything—one was the fact that though these kids' circumstances were dire, the poverty—I had never seen anything like it—everyone wanting to be adopted had a dream. They wanted to be doctors, and lawyers, and pilots. Realistically, I knew that one percent would maybe fulfill those dreams. The second fact was their love for soccer. They were able to just come alive, leave worries behind, and just be kids. One of our former beneficiaries, Buye Manisul, would often say, "When I was a kid, I would just starve, but I knew if I didn't have lunch for three days in a row, I would just eat soccer. I would just go out on the playground, and soccer would be my meal." So, seeing that passion, I thought on that plane ride home. I wrote on the back of a napkin that I wanted to build safe soccer fields because the fields I was playing on with these kids were horrible. Some fields were very slanted with barbwire surrounding them. I was pulling up glass and metal. These kids were barefoot. The playing environment was just atrocious. I knew that a big piece was bringing quality soccer programming to Uganda—and education. I started talking more and more to friends and family about this dream. Our founding board gathered in Nashville nine years ago. It was our first board or leadership summit. We discussed this dream and what this could be. We knew the education piece, but there are so many variables in education. We didn't want to assume what they needed. So, that is what we do today with the hygiene kits, with technology, and with infrastructure changes. The focus is on need, and it has been a long process. We wait until we see a need that is repeated enough times, and we address that need there.

It has been an insane journey. I just made my fortieth trip to Uganda this February and March. It has become a part of my life and my family's life. Our support system just continues to grow in such amazing ways.

ALBRECHT: So, you mentioned forty trips. When you take a trip, how long do you spend there?

WARNEKE: A typical trip is ten days, maybe seven to eight days in country. I think thirty-three days was my longest trip. In February and March, I usually do back-to-back trips. Those are our girl empowerment trips where we are distributing our hygiene kits to our mature female students, and so rather than go home and come right back, I head to Gulu in Northern Uganda, and I will drop off our team at the airport, pick up a fresh team and just stick around. So, a typical trip is ten to twelve days.

ALBRECHT: Does Abby go with you?

WARNEKE: Abby first went—we had some members that were on our founding board that were adopted from Uganda, so it was a good friend of hers from college. Her very first trip to Uganda was without me to go and support this family, just kind of stand in the gap for our friend, while her husband and kids had to return to St. Louis. Abby went and stayed with her in the middle of that. She went back with me four years ago—her first time with our organization. This last Thanksgiving our whole family went. She came over with our three boys for their first trip. It is important for our children to see this work firsthand because the more our work grows, the more I miss at home, the older they get, and the more activities I am away from. I am traveling stateside to fundraise, or when I am in Uganda, I miss a lot of stuff. We want them to understand the *why* behind that, so it was very important for them to see it. We were a little nervous with them. It is a developing world with raw poverty, but they saw kids. They just saw playmates. They saw the opportunity to kick a ball, draw on a chalkboard, and interact with kids. It was beautiful. I have taken other youth as volunteers, but certainly never as young as seven and ten.

ALBRECHT: Something stuck me as very coincidental from earlier in our conversation. Are you familiar with Katherine Switzer?

WARNEKE: No, I am not.

ALBRECHT: She was the first female to run illegally registered in the Boston Marathon, and in 2015 started a foundation called Fearless 261. One of the things we talked about was the challenges that girls face as they mature, and she is working with a company in New Zealand to create a reusable product, originally intended for athletes to help women, specifically on the continent of Africa. Her concern was that girls were missing a week of school nearly every month. She saw this as a huge inequity between male and female students. Are you seeing this problem too?

WARNEKE: It is the same in Uganda. We pretty much always use the statistic that a girl misses about thirty percent of her education when she starts her period. We were seeing that in our programs and our partner schools. We were seeing high absenteeism, and girls were not training with their soccer coaches. We asked, *why?* Well, they are on their period. That's when we began distributing kits. The first kits we began giving out about six years ago in the central region of Uganda. There is a company called Afripads that is based in Uganda. They make reusable and washable pads that last about a year. We then went to the northern region five years ago. We have given out about 10,000 kits to date. Our kits are three pair of underwear because many of these girls do not own underwear, five washable pads, a washing bucket, two bars of soap, fingernail clippers, a mirror, a comb, a washcloth—kind of some of your basic needs, but what we were realizing is we were giving these hygiene kits, but these girls were still missing school. So then, we started building changing rooms on our campuses as well. It is just a small little facility that gives these girls a dignified place to care for their needs. I love when we get to unveil these. We just did one at a school called Nabukalu in early March, and there were eighty-five moms where their kids go to this school that were there, spending the day with us praising God, overwhelmed with emotion for their daughters that they will get the dignity that they never had. They will have the joy in education that they never had. It was beautiful because you could see that the history was going to be different for these girls. Every one of these girls after these young women would not have to cower in a pit toilet or in bushes to change dirty rags.

Most of these moms had used banana leaves and old clothes in place of actual pads because they couldn't afford actual pads for their girls. You could see just a joy and a change that was taking place on these campuses. One of my favorite things that we get to do is unveil those changing rooms. Nabukalu is the eighth school that we have been able to build a changing room at, and it is a game changer for girls. Education is the other part. They need to know that it is normal, so there is signage all over those changing rooms. Those changing rooms are a big component to combatting against inequity.

In Uganda, the education there is in government-controlled schools. About twenty-two years ago, Uganda started the Universal Primary Education System—UPE schools. It is supposed to be education for all. In Uganda, the statistics change. These statistics are probably based on 2018 data. Uganda, at the time, was the second youngest nation in the world just behind Nigeria with a median age of just 15.5, so it is a nation of youth. Uganda recognized that and said that *we need to have these kids in school,* so they started government schools to combat against the private and expensive schools. However, it is free on paper but not in real life. There are hidden fees across the board for our kids. They pay for registration fees. They pay for uniforms. You get kicked out of the school if you are not wearing a uniform. You must pay exam fees and feeding fees, and so there are always hidden fees. Every school is different. It is not a universal pay. There are school management committees and PTAs at each school that decide going into each school year what that fee structure will look like. For a family that may have eight kids at home, eight dollars in school fees is insurmountable. Some of them cost probably eight to forty dollars per term, three to four terms in a year, and that's for primary. We have eight primary schools that are our primary schools. If we move to secondary schools, because of costs, we may have lost a generation. Statistics show that sixty-eight percent of those kids in those UPE schools are dropping out of school prior to graduating—basically at sixth grade. These statistics probably are not 100% accurate because Uganda is a very transitory society, so families may not be able to pay fees at one school, so they switch their kids to another school. I don't think the statistics always take that into consideration as far as a clean statistic, but regardless, at least half of the kids are not finishing primary school.

To see kids missing school and then getting what I would say is a very poor education, even at those UPE schools, is hard. We follow as many kids as we can from primary school, to secondary school, to university. That is our goal—to have these kids finish their education and walk in their dream or goal for their future. We try to give them guidance counseling on what their gifts, likes, and passions are to find a job or career filled with purpose, but we are also realistic. We have social workers on our staff, education advocates that work with all of our educational programming, soccer coaches, a health coordinator, a sustainability coordinator, our national coordinator, some drivers, and lastly some information technology professionals that take computers to schools that have no electricity. They will take them and charge them. We have Kindles all over our campuses and this device, this incredible device, called a Rachel Plus device. There is this organization that constructed this, I think that they were working mainly in Kenya at the time. It is a device with predownloaded Wikipedia, all Khan Academy videos, and different textbook materials, so we can put that on each one of our campuses. Teachers can do their research, and students can as well.

ALBRECHT: You mention poverty, but you also said that these kids you are working with have dreams. One of the things that I have noticed is some of the kids that I am working with do not have extended vision beyond their circumstances. They wouldn't even dream of becoming a doctor. Why do the kids you work with have the ability to see what is out there? What is the difference?

WARNEKE: I think that is what drew me to Uganda to begin with. I've done a lot of work with short-term mission work here in the United States, and a lot of that has been out on the reservations, and it is the same thing—kids completely, COMPLETELY, lack the ability to dream, lack the ability to think about anything but what they have seen. I think there is just this hunger in Uganda to want to rise out of poverty. So many of these kids have lived with parents in a situation where—I am going to use an example of one of our students—her name is Nantume Irene. She is one of our beneficiaries. She has actually traveled here to the United States a few times. She has spoken on behalf of girl empowerment for us. She is a teacher in Uganda. I got to see her in her classroom in February, and it was such a joy. She is one of seven kids. Her mother never had any education whatsoever—father stopped in third grade. She is in the middle of those seven children. Older siblings dropped out in late primary, early secondary. She made it to primary six. She was told by her family, "You can read. You can write your name. That's more than we can do. You're done." Thankfully, an aunt fought for her education and was able to assist. Then we stepped in to pay school fees, or she would have been married with five kids by now. But, for Irene, it is a kind of a beautiful and an almost intrinsic way of looking at things. It is not for personal gain. These people do not want to be doctors and lawyers for wealth. They want to change the system that they grew up in. They want to change, in many ways, the future for their entire family. So, Irene wants an education, but there is a pride in that because she knows that *she* can take care of her family. She can now, as a teacher of the three to four-year old class at Victory Junior School, take care of her younger siblings and pay their school fees.

Uganda is one of the most kind and sincere places I have ever been. I have not had extensive travel, but I have traveled enough to know that there is something about the people of Uganda— the resiliency, the sincerity, the kindness that allows them... if you look at their neighbors to the south, Rwanda, there was this genocide, and there was just this ability and this quickness to forgive, a quickness to look past things. In the north, where the Lord's Resistance Army planted roots for nineteen years, some of our staff members were abducted as kids, forced to be child soldiers, and everyone lived through that insurgency, what I would call a civil war. They will tell stories about how a family member was chopped up by a machete, but then they will end by saying *praise God. Someone else had it worse than I did.* They have this ability to have perspective that boggles my mind that is God-given. They have this faith. I think when you have to live by faith, which is part of poverty, that's part of Ugandan culture because you literally are praying for your next meal. You are praying for school fees for the next term. You are relying on God in a way that I don't have to, that I have never had to, growing up with parents that have loved me and a school system that has never failed me, athletics, and food in my cupboard. I have never had that need that our friends in Uganda have. I think because they are living so often by faith, that idea of hope or idea of dreaming for a future is easier to attain because of the faith component that is already there. That's the only thing I can say because I've dealt with kids, even here in the poor county that live in Missouri that are in 'the system' and are content being in the system. The beauty of struggle, the beauty of poverty, is it makes you more resilient. It gives you the ability to problem solve. You know, you put my own three boys in the lives of the kids in Uganda, they are throwing in the towel on day one because it is too hard, and they haven't been forced to kind of figure things out. So, I think because of all those dynamics, it allows these kids in a beautiful way to dream for a better tomorrow. I often tell our volunteers before they come to Uganda, you can look at scripture, and you can look at Jesus talking about the least of these, but these are not the kids he is talking about. These are some of the greatest kids on planet Earth. They have more faith than you will understand and have learned what it means to rely on God for everything. So, I think that leads to the ability to dream.

ALBRECHT: Wow, so what I am hearing is having less is often having more. Correct?

WARNEKE: Absolutely! We have the poverty of having too much. That is not a quote by me. I can't remember the book I read it out of many, many years ago. We are so distracted. Perhaps this time of social distancing and being kind of quarantined to home is allowing us to maybe understand that we are drowning in our own stuff a little bit. Maybe, this will be freeing from that. Yup, we have the poverty of too much, and I think social media is there in Uganda but not to the level it is here. Our teens [in the United States], that comparison trap, that they are always comparing themselves to someone else, there is still a little bit of freedom for kids in Uganda. When you pull up to a school, kids in Uganda will sing and dance for you just as a guest. There is a respect, a kindness, and a lack of shame. Whereas some kids that can't sing well will still sing, but kids in the United States will not sing. They are going to hide in the shadows, or a kid that can't draw very well gives up on that early, whereas in Uganda there is this ability and not a shame in having to be the best. There is still joy in just the dancing and the singing, which we have lost a little bit here.

- **2** -

I HAVE A few favorite country roads. When I run, I notice the garbage sitting on the roadside or the drainage ditch. There are a lot of litterbugs. I live in New York State. Here, we have a five-cent deposit on all plastic and tin beverage containers. One day it hit me—*all these bottles and cans on the side of the road have a deposit.* The next day I walked the ten-mile stretch. At the end of the day, I was $46.25 wealthier. In about three hours, I had collected 925 containers. That road is only one of hundreds in my area. The poverty of having too much is a real problem that is disrupting hope.

School is an equalizer. Where I teach, if a student does not reveal it, and there isn't gross negligence on their caregiver's part, most students do not know who is poor and who comes from wealthier homes. More and more kids from wealthy families are struggling emotionally. Schools are slow to act upon challenges when students are doing well academically. These students are clean and well put together. A new form of abuse has developed with the increase of distractions. The consequences of this abuse are further reaching and catastrophic to hope and purpose. Kids are getting ignored. Opportunities to be distracted from loving and caring for our own families are on the rise. A family who moves in the right or wrong direction still learns by consequence; however, when a family fails to develop at all, nothing is learned because they are metaphorically suspended in time. Where there is no learning, there is no development of hope or purpose.

Warneke claimed that the United States has "the poverty of having too much," though he admitted that he could not remember what he was quoting. Distractions in today's world are everywhere—cellphones, multiple forms of messaging, complex jobs, social media, and an overstimulation of instant information. People that have a lot of material things and complex and busy lives can easily forgo working on hope. The proof is on the side of the road; one nickel at a time, people are tossing their money out of car windows.

Hope is not developed instantaneously. Like the crack of a whip, the snap is heard after the whip is swung. Many families are distracted by *the poverty of having too much*. Their poverty is a lack of hope and purpose passed off from one generation to the next because they are too immersed in their distractions.

Early in my interview with Warneke he stated, "If you can't believe that tomorrow can be better than today, then we have given up." If a person is getting a handout, but not being asked to work, what seems like a beautiful thing is quite damaging. It erases hope because a person who sees tomorrow just like today lacks a sense of purpose. They are not learning or developing because their discovery of hope and purpose is ignored. Handouts do that. Warneke himself said that, "You can just see a physical change in these kids when they finally believe that tomorrow has some potential in it." There is hesitation in the United States for people to ask those in need to work or serve others. A person who lacks money should know the joy of serving another person. There is an educational value and a discovery of purpose through service. The financially poor may need material support, but more vital to their development of hope and purpose is a need for empowerment. If this does not come with the handout, we are putting Band-Aids on wounds that do not heal.

Can a hairbrush save a life? As educators, it is impossible to fill the void of a challenging home life. It does not take long for classrooms to feel like second families, and where there is a need, so many teachers go out of their way to help. When teachers shop, we often think of our own students in the same way that we think about our own families. A number of years ago, JoJo bows were in style, but at the beginning of the year one of my girls did not have the hair ribbons, ties, or bows that her peers had. Her unclean hair badly needed to be cut. She was eight years old, and fully aware of the way she looked. She acted out and never did her homework. Her apathy at home carried over into school, but she also was attention starved. There was frequent drug use in the home. Schools do not provide haircuts, but it is an essential practice to treat every student with respect and dignity. It is hard to do when that student is not respectful.

I took a chance and bought a hairbrush and a few hairclips with bows. They were nothing fancy. Away from the other students, my classroom aide and I took turns daily brushing the girl's hair. We talked while we brushed. Sometimes she talked about home, other times we talked about the future. There were silent days too, and others that we were pushed to the point of frustration. Progress can be slow. The conversations revealed that this girl had little ability to see past the current day. As Warneke explained, if we are going to make progress, all people need to know their purpose in this world. We continued to hold our student accountable, but we interwove that with time to develop dignity and help her discover hope and purpose. Children act out, stay sad, or sometimes even are resilient by nature when they are ignored. As those children grow older, sustained periods of time where a person is ignored rear uglier consequences. Teen pregnancy? Repeated generational poverty? Substance abuse? Suicide? Teachers do not have crystal balls, but it is better to try anything, even if it is the wrong thing, than stay in a standstill.

The brush and hair clips were bought in November. We bought lice medicine in December, but as hard as it was to deal with smells, parasites, and greasy hair, we brushed that girl's hair every day. Being moral may involve a risk. Brushing a student's hair is unconventional. Did it cure everything? No. She had years of hopelessness behind her, and that could not be cured in a matter of seven months of school. However, as poor as her homework looked, by March, she was doing it on her own. Pride came with that. By April she was taking it upon herself to bathe, and though I enjoyed the conversations while brushing her hair, she began doing it herself. Small things have the potential to create bends in a person's life path.

Like many high schools in America, ours has a Key Club. To belong, students must maintain a certain number of volunteer hours. This is troubling. Relegating community service to a set number of hours is analogous with checking off a box or simply adding a resume builder. Can a minimum standard be developed when developing service mindedness? Service is a lifestyle, not a series of moments in time. The concept of an on/off switch being applied to service is contradictory to the development of a life-style. In order to create a society of selfless people, the pattern of service needs to start before the first days of kindergarten, so by the time students are high schoolers, service is as natural as breathing.

Six years after that little girl left our classroom, a junior in high school walked into my room. She was maintaining a C average. It was my former student. Her hair still needed attention, but it was clean and brushed. She had found her love—volunteering at a local nursing home. She talked to me about it for a long time and dropped a bombshell on that visit. She said that her Key Club requirements were to go and sit with older people, do a puzzle or a game, or simply talk to them for a paltry eight hours per semester. She recognized that this was not what the people needed. On her own, she bought each of the ladies a hairbrush and began brushing their hair when she visited. She said that it was a lot easier to get an older person to talk if she simply brushed their hair. She was not pregnant, was still in school, and was passing. Is it possible that brushing dirty, lice-infested hair saved a life? Two years later, I was asked to read names at graduation. As fate would have it, I read her name. I have not heard from her since, but I know one thing—a girl graduated because she saw her purpose in life. Serving others gave her hope and purpose.

How much different is a hairbrush from feminine hygiene kits? Both were given to people that needed them, but they were given by people who said that a free handout needs to be given with the gift of education. Throwing money at a problem destroys hope and purpose unless that realization is in place. In February and March, Warneke's Field of Dreams focuses on women and their equality with men. Early on, they realized that women were not attending school or soccer practice during their period. Due to poverty, women had no way to stay sanitary. To avoid embarrassment, they just stayed home. Inequity in education and sports was a result of a biological difference. Money was spent wisely on reusable products, but they did not anticipate this would have no effect on attendance. If the volunteers were not there to witness it themselves, how would they know that this phenomenon was happening? To effectively serve other human beings, the service providers must provide tools and education on using the tools, as well as stick around to see if the plan works. This is where philanthropy sometimes misses the mark. In Warneke's case, he and his team stayed and observed the results of their efforts. Though it seemed like a simple conclusion that giving out products and education would fix the problem, the Field of Dreams team learned that something else was lacking. Women needed a private facility to care for themselves.

If hope is to be developed successfully, what is put in place needs to be sustainable. Sustainability is attained by imparting education, but how can a person get an education if they are attending class only seventy percent of the time? If hope is built through hard work, and a person is trapped in their own hut because of natural biology, hope is stifled. Toward the end of Michael Warneke's interview, he referred to the importance of people not feeling shame. Like the girl in my class, shame was stifling a sense of purpose like the Ugandan women. To truly know how a person is feeling, it is necessary to devote a lot of time to that soul. Shame does not always present itself explicitly. People with genuine concern must maintain a lifestyle of service, and through that true growth can take root.

- 3 -

THE MORE A person serves others, the more they are able to discover their hope and purpose. Is service mindedness a skill that needs to be taught, or is it simply a natural function that just needs to be tapped into? Is service one of the basic instincts of life? A symbiotic relationship between plants and fungi may shed some light on the nature of people.

Mycorrhizal networks are living underground connections

that involve a mutually beneficial link between fungi and plants. Though currently understudied, the joint behavior of two different living kingdoms has a lot to teach people about the discovery of hope and purpose. The roots of different species of plants are not connected directly, but they are associated by a fungal network. Plants need nutrients and minerals from the soil such as nitrogen, potassium, phosphorus, and an extensive list of many trace elements. Nutrients are not equally distributed in soil, and it would take plants a lot of energy to send out unnecessary roots in random searches. This is where the fungi come into play. Fungi are different than the roots of plants; they spread out quickly and naturally. By their innate design, fungi are much more efficient than plants at circulating out in the soil. Ectomycorrhizal fungi attach themselves to the root tips of trees and plants guiding them to nutrients, while receiving energy from the plant. This symbiotic relationship allows both plants and fungi to flourish.

One fungus can connect to multiple plants, and one plant can work with multiple fungi. The fungi regulate the transport of nutrients from one plant to another. A fungus can even lead a plant's roots to water. In pine forests, trees may all look similar, but they can have vast differences in age and health. Some trees that look healthy at first glance may look dead beyond the needles, while other trees look healthy all around. This is because, through the reaction of the fungi in the soil, the neighboring trees will keep a struggling tree alive by pumping nutrients though the mycorrhizal network. The surrounding trees give up their nutrients to provide life support to the struggling tree. A tree will suffer to keep a less fortunate tree alive based on the guidance of fungi. Since certain fungi react to enzymes specific to the roots of one species, fungi will often focus on connections between similar plants, though there are exceptions. Evergreen Douglass firs have been connected to deciduous birch trees. In this relationship, the trees require different seasonal nutrients, so they trade off nutrients based on the time of year. Through exchanges made within the mycorrhizal networks, trees are healthier and have a greater resistance to disease than if they lived alone or solely with their own species. Living in diverse groups creates greater resilience than one individual could achieve.

Using these relationships to say that all living things are pre-programmed to serve is, admittedly, quite a leap. Mycorrhizal networks look vastly different from human relationships. But the connection between trees and their communication through a fungi network does prove that humans are not the sole species on Earth that understand the relationship of give and take. Trees and fungi are not distracted by material ownership, jobs, or the countless challenges that people face. Their sole desire is to survive and produce the seed of the next generation.

Essentially, plants and fungi may live entirely undistracted. They develop slowly, and each action of a tree is highly efficient. Yet, a tree is willing to compromise and share nutrients at its own expense to assist neighboring trees, even those of other species. If all the distractions of human life that are deemed unnecessary were to be taken away, very few necessities are left for survival— food, creating new life, and the human need for hope and love. If the necessity for food and love comes to the neediest people by way of other people, how different are humans from trees? The superfluous elements that consume many people's days cloud basic living instinct. Service is an ingredient that exists within the balance of the natural world, and it is not unique to humans. To understand humanity's place within the living world, distractions must be removed. Simplification leads to service, which allows people to discover their hope and purpose.

On September 9th, 2007, one of my father's stories arrived. He wrote about his mother's actions during the Second World War. With his father stationed on the Russian front, my father was raised solely by his mom. She had three boys born in 1931, 1933 and 1935 and did not know if or when her husband was returning home. What was it like for a sort of single mom during that time? Did she have to break the rules of conventional thought to maintain order in the household during challenging times? In my father's words:

I remember the war years. There was Muttle [his mother] with a seven-year-old boy, a five-year-old one and me, a real handful for a four-year-old. You know, it was not easy to feed and clothe the family. She always found something for herself and for us. All week long during the spring, summer, and the fall, we wore our lederhosen. Sometimes they had to be washed. We hated this because afterwards the leather was stiff, and the lederhosen had to be broken in again. On Sundays we wore shorts, which Muttle made from various remnants and from old uniforms which Vatle [his father] brought home during his short once a year leave. Toward the end of the war, Gerhard [my father's brother] needed a shirt. But there was not material or old shirts for sewing available. Since it was law that each family had to have a national flag, a swastika flag, in the house, Muttle felt pretty safe and colored the entire flag red. The largest portion of the flag was already red. However, the black swastika could still be seen. So, Muttle made the shirt out of the flag anyway. The swastika was on the shirt in the back near his rear end, below the belt line. I wish that I still had that shirt!

Socks were impossible to buy. Muttle had knit all our socks. Holes in socks naturally happened. Muttle wanted to repair the socks when the holes were small. Boys tend to wait a long time to report holes in their socks. There was a time I waited way too long. To avoid the wrath of Muttle, I taught myself to mend the socks. I did a darn good job, I remember.

One year, Muttle bought carrots. That food was readily available. She bought over two hundred pounds and prepared them so that we could eat carrots throughout the winter. We had carrots, more carrots and even more carrots. We got tired of it. But what these carrots did was most astonishing. We all looked healthy and had a "tan." The doctor told Muttle that it was probably from eating all those carrots. Eggs were impossible to get. Muttle went to farmers in the area, people she knew, and begged for us. The farmers had eggs, but eggs were 'under control' and a certain amount of eggs and milk had to be delivered to the town hall for ultimate delivery to the front troops.

It was about 1942 when Vatle met two young Russian sisters. They asked Vatle if he could arrange for them to get away from the frontline and go to Germany. Vatle thought about it and sent one, Katja, to us and her sister, Natja, to some friends in a neighboring town. Katja and Muttle understood each other very well. Katja did not speak any German when she first arrived. She was a great help to Muttle and us boys. Under the Third Reich, any Jewish people or Russians, such as Katja, had to wear a special identification on their clothing when they were away from the house. After the occupation came, the only people allowed in the street were the people with the special ID. Katja used this privilege to help us. Muttle talked often about Katja after she left. Toward the end of the war, Katja had a boyfriend, a Russian prisoner of war. When all POWs were freed, both went back together. We never heard from her again. When I was in Switzerland, I asked the Red Cross in Geneva if they could search for Katja. They said that it could be done but suggested not to do this. The Cold War could *create many difficulties for Katja. It would show a connection to the west.*

My grandmother had to break the rules to survive. Her devotion to serve her children gave her that strength. Each person gets one life, so if survival is your reason for breaking the rules, it makes sense. She had a friend, a young Russian girl named Katja. Though she did not break legal rules, I am sure there were more than a few eyebrows raised in town when my grandmother took in Katja. Rule breakers challenge our concept of what is possible, and that strength to serve others is a superhighway toward the discovery of hope and purpose.

Chapter 4
Share the Mountains That People Can't Climb

"Have an open mind and keep learning-
be interested in learning."
-Quang-Tuan Luong, Photographer, California

- 1 -

On March 1st, 1872, a large thermal area of land located in the northwest section of Wyoming was designated as the first national park—Yellowstone. There are sixty-two national parks that have been designated by the United States Congress. In addition, over 350 national monuments have been created by an executive order of the President of the United States. The mission of the United States Park Service is to "preserve the natural and cultural resources and the values of the National Park System for the enjoyment, education, and inspiration of this and future generations." Does the natural world and the preservation of places of historical significance influence the rediscovery of hope and purpose? What if a person is not physically or financially able to get to a park? Can the parks still play a role in a person's growth?

Quang-Tuan (QT) Luong was born to Vietnamese parents and raised in France. At a young age, the challenge and beauty of the Alps led him to become a mountain climber and a wilderness guide. Realizing that not everybody can scale mountain peaks and see their grandeur, he felt a mission to give every person on the planet the opportunity to see these places of incredible beauty. Luong's photography started as a hobby. Luong has since been all over the world and has become one of the most recognized photographers of the twenty-first century. He has summited the coldest mountaintops on the planet and has photographed in the warmest of tropical waters.

QT Luong came to the United States to work in the field of artificial intelligence, but his hobby of sharing the mountains through photography would redirect his life's work. Luong has a Ph.D. from the University of Paris. Upon seeing California's Yosemite Valley, Luong developed a love for the National Parks of the United States. This began a turning point in his life. With a seventy-five-pound backpack filled with photography equipment, Luong set out on a mission to visit and photograph all of America's national parks. By 2002, he had visited and photographed all fifty-eight of the national parks becoming the first person to do so. (Since then, four new parks have been designated.) In 2009, Ken Burns and Dayton Duncan featured Luong and his work in the Public Broadcasting series "The National Parks: America's Best Idea." Luong's photographs have appeared in National Geographic, Time, Life, Scientific American, Outside, and hundreds of other magazines. He also has four large-scale books and has received numerous awards for his work in photography.

Is there a connection between service and the discovery of hope and purpose? Can a person completely change careers in their prime and still make progress living a joyful life? Luong's words speak truth to the consistent reason he began photographing the world in the first place. The sound of his voice is cheerful with a thick French accent, along with the calmness and reflection of a man who speaks as if each word carries a precious meaning.

ALBRECHT: Thank you for agreeing to talk with me. I first became familiar with you when I saw your work and accomplishments on Ken Burns's series on the national parks. You have an unusual history. Would you describe your history?

LUONG: Well, you know, I started—you probably want to know how I got into photography, right? So, I was actually born in Paris from Vietnamese parents, and I was pretty much raised as a city kid. But, my work, it changed, while I was in the university. School and college friends took me up to hike the peaks of the Alps. It was a mountaineering club, a university mountaineering club, and then I discovered the wilderness for the first time. I made the connection with nature up there, and I started to take up mountaineering as a hobby. Subsequently, I took up photography in order to bring back to the folks who couldn't go up there, the beauty of the high mountains. So, that is how I started photography.

ALBRECHT: You originally started photography for other people, correct?

LUONG: Yes.

ALBRECHT: You were not being trained as a photographer and were pursuing a Ph.D. in artificial intelligence. Now you are a professional photographer. Was this a difficult transition?

LUONG: It is something that came about after a fair amount of years in research. I was initially trained as a scientist, and the reason I came to America was out of pure curiosity. I just wanted to come here to see what it would be [like] to live and work in America. Initially, I had the position, which was as a post-doctoral researcher with the intention to go back to France after that, but then I began to visit America's national parks, and I wanted to go see more of them. So, that is why I eventually sought a job in the United States instead of coming back to France, and so I held that job from between 1995 to 2007, for about twelve years. The reason I chose a job in California in Silicon Valley is that I saw that it would afford me more free time to do my travels to the national parks. Starting in the early 2000s, I began to reduce the number of my working hours, and eventually worked part-time.

It was kind of a graduate position for me.

ALBRECHT: Was it a challenge to take that final leap of faith and go full-time into photography?

LUONG: I would say twelve years ago it was a bit easier than it is today. In the intervening years, it is becoming more increasingly challenging to make a living in photography, but I was doing fairly well actually then. I was doing fairly well, so it was not too difficult. My wife was very worried about that because this was our source of income, and she was right, actually.

ALBRECHT: What drew you to the national parks of the United States? You were in Europe. You have the Alps and many beautiful parks there.

LUONG: It is really the diversity. In Europe, all the wilderness we have left is basically the mountaintops. Everything that is below this is at the table and has been habituated. However, here, in the Americas, the national parks, they encompass at the scale of the continent, so you have deserts, vast forest—everything from the tropics to the arctic. So, really the diversity of nature of the national parks is what fascinated me.

ALBRECHT: So, what is or has been your greatest challenge? You have been to all national parks. Is this true, that you visited all of the national parks?

LUONG: Yes, and actually I have visited each park many times, so on average I have visited each of them about five times or more.

ALBRECHT: Incredible! Do you have a favorite?

LUONG: Based on the visits, that would be difficult to say. Each park is so different, but I would say for sentimental reasons, it would have to be Yosemite because that was the first park I visited, but when I was living in France, I knew nothing about the United States national parks. I remember that I was doing a lot of climbing and mountaineering, and climbers tell me *you go to this* *place, there are incredible rock walls to climb.* So, of all the great research universities, I chose Berkley because it was the closest to Yosemite. That really is the park that brought me to here, in California, and I visited it more than any of the other parks I have had other visits at.

ALBRECHT: Do you plan on staying in that area?

LUONG: Yeah, I am settled now here in San Jose, you know. I am married. We have two children. We have a house here, so we will be here for a while, I suppose.

ALBRECHT: So, greatest challenge, other than money... what would be one of the greatest challenges you faced as a photographer?

LUONG: Well, for me, after I started a family, to advance time away from the family, time in the field and the time spent with the family.

ALBRECHT: You described the natural world, but your self-written autobiography describes that you *celebrate human heritage.* How do you define *celebrating human heritage*?

LUONG: Well, you know, it means mostly that I am interested in finding beauty in the world, so recently I have gotten more attention for my works in the national parks and the American landscape. Before that, I was interested in seeing the beauty in all the cultures in the world. I travel extensively abroad, mostly in Asia and some of the countries as well.

ALBRECHT: As a teacher, I have a personal investment and interest in children. If you had to teach children or give one lesson to children, or one thought that you think is a *must* that children should know, what would it be?

LUONG: [very long pause]

ALBRECHT: Perhaps we will come back to that question. Let me ask you this. Have you had a teacher that stands out in your life as an influential teacher?

LUONG: Yes, he was a history teacher—a high school history teacher. He had a way that helped make sense of history and give meaning to it. Oh, that was at my school in Paris.

ALBRECHT: So, thinking back to my initial question. What would you say is the most important thing that should be considered when teaching people, especially children?

LUONG: I would say that the most important part of a school would be to inspire the students to have an open mind and keep learning and be interested in learning.

ALBRECHT: How would you define yourself as a person at the point that you are at in your life?

LUONG: [another long pause] I am someone who is out in the world and tried to understand its beauty and complexity. I tried to communicate a little bit of that of what I have learned to others.

- 2 -

WHEN I CONTACTED Quang-Tuan Luong, my research indicated that his life story connected best with serving others. He climbs mountains, travels to remote areas, and brings what he sees in the form of pictures to people who would never be able to see these landscapes otherwise. Service to others fills a void in another person's life. His pictures allow people to see the unreachable. However, Luong's interview revealed an alternative and powerful lens behind his work. We only get one life, and what you do with your life nets hope in yourself and the people we all serve. Luong holds a Ph.D. from the University of Paris and was researching artificial intelligence at Berkley. For this type of work, intelligence, creativity, and work ethic all must cross paths, and this is why highly paid people live comfortably if they are working in Silicon Valley. Luong was on the path to what people would view as a highly successful career. Why would he change?

Anna Mary Robertson was born on September 7th, 1860. The third of ten children, she was inspired to paint at a very young age. She attended school in Bennington, Vermont, and due to a shortage of supplies, the young girl painted with grape juice, ground grass, ochre, and paste from flour. However, like most girls of this period, school ceased far too soon, and at the age of twelve, Robertson would leave her home to work as a cook, seamstress, and housekeeper for fifteen years. At age twenty-seven, she would marry Thomas Moses, and the two of them would have ten children. They raised their children in the Shenandoah Valley and eventually settled permanently on a farm in Eagle Bridge, New York.

Anna Moses's husband would die at the age of sixty-seven, and in 1936, she would move into her daughter's home. Though only five of her children survived to adulthood, there were many children and family members around her, and nearly everybody began to refer to her as *Mother Moses* or *Grandma Moses*. Grandma Moses was an avid quilter and enjoyed needlepoint, but arthritis began making this hobby more and more painful. At the age of seventy-eight, as needlepoint became increasingly difficult, her childhood love of painting reemerged. She traded needlepoint materials for a paintbrush. As she recalled in her autobiography: "I was quite small. My father would get me and my brothers white paper by the sheet. He liked to see us draw pictures. It was a penny a sheet and lasted longer than candy."

Grandma Moses began her painting career by capturing scenes of rural life from her memory. She described her scenes as *old-timey* New England landscapes. Further on in her book, Moses said she would "get an inspiration and start painting; then I'll forget everything, everything except how things used to be and how to paint it, so people will know how we used to live." Between age seventy-eight and her death at the age of one hundred and one, Grandma Moses produced over 1,500 oil paintings, which in her early years she sold for three to five dollars. By 1939, Grandma Moses's works were included in an exhibition at the New York Museum of Modern Art. Further expositions followed, and when Grandma Moses was present, she would bring her own baked goods to sell to the attendees. A decade later, President Harry Truman handed her the Women's National Press trophy. When she died in December of 1961, President John F. Kennedy spoke these words:

> The directness and vividness of her paintings restored a primitive freshness to our perception of the American scene. Both her work and her life helped our nation renew its pioneer heritage and recall its roots in the countryside and on the frontier. All Americans mourn her loss.

It is human nature for people to come to a crossroads in their lives where only bold action and fearlessness will develop growth. Wealth and possessions are useless at the end, but the way a life is lived will put the rubber stamp on hope and purpose. It would be sad if a person's dying words were *woulda', coulda', shoulda'.* Fear of instability and failure sets boundaries, but there are also times where people need to break the rules and take a leap of faith. QT Luong had to make a decision. Though his transition to photography of the natural world did not develop into a career overnight, his decision to remove the obstacle of a highly technical job to purse his purpose and passion as a photographer is bold. He had a steady income and a place to live. Essentially, he was locked into a career. Most people are. We train children to follow their dreams, but the reality of the world must be that money is the exchange medium that allows most people to have a roof over their heads and food on the table. Some passions do not line up with gainful employment. If the pressure of money is something you want to avoid, there are times in which people must compromise their passions.

Even in the most intense careers, people do have free time. This is the place that dreams need to be cultivated. Like Grandma Moses, Luong used his free time to unleash a dream held deep within. Luong was unconventional. He left the stability of a Ph.D. and work in Silicon Valley to travel the path of a photographer in the national parks. How much different is this from Grandma Moses starting a painting career at the age of seventy-eight? The stories are not all that different from each other.

Distractions such as television, the internet, and various other time-consuming or mindless activities are highly addictive. If you are unhappy, ask yourself: are you pursuing your dreams in your free time? Luong did. He went to his job, but when he had time on his hands, he traveled to Yosemite. A snowball effect occurs as people work hard to stay focused on their dreams. Dreams grow into lifestyles, and if you are as fortunate as QT Luong, an opportunity may present itself to pair your passion and your livelihood. Suddenly, a life of hope and purpose will become a full-time lifestyle, and the concept of work melts away. Is it easy? No. The world we live in is full of distractions and people who want to tell us what to do with our free time. Take it back. Your life is your life. Do not let it be crippled through the submission to gadgets or others.

No person can own another person, but QT Luong and Grandma Moses remind us that there are physical constraints in the world. To put food on the table and a roof over your family's head require an income. It is rare for a passion to lead to sustainable income right off the bat. Whether a person's dreams include sports or art, a very lucky few start out their careers doing exactly what they would like to do for the rest of their lives. Most people get up each day and go to work at a job where they have little control over what they do and when they choose to do it. At the end of the workday, a choice exists. Binge watching Netflix, overeating, surfing Facebook, and several other highly addictive distractions are waiting for you the moment you open the door to your home.

The pursuit of a purpose in life is associated with passions and dreams. Each person's vision is as unique as a fingerprint. At first thought, why would a person not come home to their free time and follow their dreams? There is hard work when pursuing a dream, and whether obligations or distractions are at home, a person must make a conscious decision to chase their dream and purpose if he or she is going to have hope. If you want hope in your life, you are going to have to make a conscious decision, and it may be at odds with how most people spend their free time. Grandma Moses's example illustrates how no person is ever too old to start pursuing a change. Quan-Tang Luong sheds light on the importance of never losing sight of what we are called to do. In reading Luong's self-published autobiography, he does not live a pampered life. He lugs his own heavy equipment miles into the wilderness. It is punishing work, and as sure as Grandma Moses aged, there had to be days where it would have been quite easy to say *not today* to their canvasses. Both stayed steadfast. Hope is attainable, but do not expect it to be easily realized.

- **3** -

THE PICTURES FROM our Christmas Eve in 2018 look just like any other year. I am wearing the same red sweater vest and black pants I have worn for about a decade. I loathe buying new clothing, even if it is out of style. I am a lot like my father, who still wears the same llama wool sweater I gave him in 1992. My boys are in the same ties, my daughter has a red dress, and my stepmother is in one of those big loose turtleneck sweaters—the same thing every year. Even our dog, Harley, gets in on the action. He is stylish with a new bandana every year. So, the extent of changing the family wardrobe comes down to cutting a triangle of fabric. Other than hairstyles, I would say that there is no difference in the way the pictures look from one year to the next—except 2018.

The 2018 edition of Christmas Eve photos looks more like a dentist office. First off, my middle son Cory got ahold of the camera. That was mistake number one. He does not know how to keep his finger off the shutter button. My kids grew up in the digital camera era, so they do not know the feeling of moderation that a twenty-four-photo roll of film instilled in me. The scene looked something like this: Dad was trying his hardest to fill a tube up with saliva, and I was scraping the inside of my mouth with a very abrasive tool to stick in some liquid. 2018 was the year I decided once and for all to covertly confirm I was not adopted. My dad is bald, and I am not. My blood type does not match my parents. I love athletics; my parents hate to sweat. So, for Christmas 2018, I gave my dad a DNA kit. I also bought one for myself. The kits came from two different companies. I removed every variable. It was time to find out some dirt. Two months later the tests came back, and the data revealed I am nearly a clone of my dad. The panic of male pattern baldness set in.

The simple idea that I just did not drop out of the sky was gone, but something unexpected was revealed. My father was born in Germany, and as far as our family tree traces back, our lineage has remained in that country. As shown on the copper sheeting on Ellis Island embossed with every immigrant that ever walked through the facility, I am two nationalities: German and Italian. The results of the DNA tests begged to differ.

Initially, the tests showed that two migrations out of eastern Africa is where *my people* originated from 44,000 years ago (from my German grandmother) and 120,000 years ago (from my German grandfather). This did not surprise me because I have read enough National Geographic magazines to know where most scientists believe that human beings originated. However, here was the big bombshell: our test results revealed that I am 61% French, 21% Slavic, 17% Spanish and only 1% Italian. No German! Impossible! One week later my dad's results came back. His numbers were similar.

The United States is the great melting pot of the world. America is a unique country with pockets of almost every nationality of people immigrating by choice or bound into slavery from all regions of the Earth. On Christmas Eve 2018, as my father and I looked like deranged patients over the kitchen sink in a dentist office, I learned something. People of long ago were highly mobile. Of course, they did not have cars or planes, so the migration of the human species did not happen as fast as it does today. But the truth is, from the first time that homo sapiens walked the Earth, people have been on the move.

Thor and Liv Heyerdahl were on the adventure of a lifetime. The year was 1937, and this Norwegian couple had traveled nearly halfway around the world to study biology, tour, and relax on the Polynesian island of Fatu Hiva. Both Thor and Liv were successful zoologists. They were there to collect specimens of wildlife and make detailed observations of the unique island habitat.

Of course, work came with pleasure, so the couple also spent time relaxing, especially in the northern cove of the island where isolated sandy beaches expose the contrast of ocean joining together with drastic volcanic cliffs.

Like many of the Polynesian islands, there is evidence of humans having lived there for hundreds or perhaps thousands of years. Large Tiki and giant Moai sculptures of god-like heads are common on the islands. The more Thor Heyerdahl delved into the biology of Fata Hiva, the greater his curiosity became about where the first inhabitants of the island came from. French Polynesia is hundreds of miles south of Hawaii and 4,000 miles away from Peru. Without planes or modern boats, how would people have managed such a voyage?

Thor and Liv continued to collect specimens from the challenging terrain of Fata Hiva. The couple explored Omo'a, the southernmost bay on the western coast of Fatu Hiva. This is the best place to anchor and most likely is where the Álvaro de Mendaña expedition would have chosen to land. The first recorded sighting of Fatu Hiva by the Europeans was by the Spanish expedition of Mendaña on July 21st, 1595. However, this voyage was well financed and fortified. Their boats were built to withstand the fierce Pacific Ocean.

Today, this paradise has a small population. A 2002 census of the village at the bay of Omo'a showed that there were only 247 inhabitants. The valley of Omo'a is well-watered and curves in a half-moon shape, first to the southeast, and then to the northeast, terminating at the island's central plateau. This is where Thor Heyerdahl and his wife came ashore in 1937, an experience recorded in his book, *Fatu Hiva: Back to Nature*. Five hundred years ago, the only recorded boats that were as seaworthy as Mendaña's came from Europe. No boats from South America or

Asia are known, so how did people come to be on this island? Thor Heyerdahl researched all known documentation and other expeditions that visited Fata Hiva. He noted that the natives used small fishing rafts that seemed no different to what they were using in the 1930s. The question tugged at Heyerdahl like an itch that just could not be scratched. Heyerdahl was an experienced traveler and had also spent time in Peru. He thought at length about how similar the pyramids and temples found on the coast of Peru were to those in Polynesia. Could there be a connection?

A legend in Peru existed that light-skinned people lived there led by a man named Kon Tiki, or the son of the Sun. These people worshiped the sun god, and a conflict with the Incas caused them to be driven out of Peru. Much of the 15th century explorers' documentation was their astonishment of how light skinned and bearded the people of Fata Hiva were. Heyerdahl was convinced that the inhabitants of this small island, 4,000 miles from Peru, were descended from people who traveled by small rafts halfway across the Pacific. Like QT Luong, and Grandma Moses, Heyerdahl decided to stop his research because he had to answer that burning question.

Using his observations and documentation, he concluded that the original inhabitants crossed 4,000 miles of ocean on a raft. He took his idea to many places but was met only with scorn. He visited some of the best scholars on Polynesian culture in New York City; nobody wanted to finance or spend time working on his idea. Breakthroughs in biological testing did not exist at the time, and Heyerdahl believed in his theory. Like Luong, his pursuit went against the grain of common practice. Every person has a different set of interests. As obscure as the obsession to discover the origins of Fatu Hiva's inhabitants was, its answer was important to one individual—Heyerdahl.

What if Heyerdahl did not pursue his idea and just kept plugging away at his job as a zoologist? Would the world be different? Probably not. Likewise, had QT Luong not made a complete change in the direction of his career path, only a small sliver of the photography world would look different. Facing naysayers or bucking trends is rarely about changing the world. In most circumstances, adversity happens in our day to day lives. Had Heyerdahl stayed down after being told his idea was absurd, the world would have gone on, but what about Thor Heyerdahl himself? Would his life have been lived to its full potential? Would he ever have discovered his hope and purpose? He certainly would never have had the opportunity to test his theory.

The impact and western discovery of what would become known as the Kon Tiki raft is remarkable. Heyerdahl put everything he had into testing whether a raft could be seaworthy over a duration of time facing the harsh weather of the Pacific. He needed thick skin to face the naysayers. It is not easy, yet those who are able to do it create their own purpose in life. It was nobody's responsibility to support Thor Heyerdahl's theory. There are always going to be those that question ideas, shoot down visionaries, or talk behind a person's back just to do it. People who want hope and purpose live with it and do their best not to let others rewrite their vision.

Thor Heyerdahl was a man of hope. Shortly after World War II, while in New York City, he met a Norwegian engineer named Herman Watzinger. Watzinger was a veteran of the Second World War and highly educated. The two began to lay out plans for the construction of a raft using only the technologies and materials available to the people of pre-Columbian eras. All the construction was based off records and illustrations made by the conquistadors. This meant that most of the craft was to be constructed out of balsa wood. As a Boy Scout my troop constructed everything out of balsa wood because it is easy to carve and lightweight. It also snaps easily. Heyerdahl recruited a full crew for the raft, with each member possessing a necessary skill. The raft left Peru on April 28th, 1947. 4,300 miles of ocean later, the raft smashed into a reef in French Polynesia. The crew had been at sea unsupported for 102 days. They proved that a raft made of balsa wood could carry people all the way to these remote Pacific islands. Heyerdahl did not change the world, but he did take charge of his own world.

Technology has changed the way we problem solve. Would the Kon Tiki raft have ever been constructed or tried had simple DNA tests been around in the 1930s? Probably not. DNA testing of those people who are of Polynesian descent revealed years later that seventy-nine percent are Asian and twenty-one percent Melanesian. Based on modern science, Polynesians are mainly a part of a migration settled between 3000 and 1000 BC by people from Taiwan, the Philippines, and parts of New Guinea. Modern science disproved Thor Heyerdahl's theory about a group of people making their way by raft from Peru, but does that really matter? Heyerdahl's hypothesis was incorrect, but in hope and purpose he was one hundred percent correct. In the scheme of life, he faced his naysayers and fulfilled his purpose. It is a basic human right to discover hope and purpose, but it requires work, confidence in a quest, and the inner strength to change life's direction.

Chapter 5
One Lives When One Fails

"Take small bites."

-Ken Deardorff

- 1 -

My cellphone simply vibrates in the next room, and I know that a text message has come in. I forgot to turn off the ringer. Now I have two choices: get up or ignore it. The phone is in the kitchen. I am in bed. It is 1:00 AM. Curiosity has me awake in bed, but if I get up, sleep is over too. Later that day, I am teaching, and the cell phone buzzes in my pocket. Am I present in the moment? It is natural to wonder who is texting me. Modern America, staying plugged in—does it have to be 24-7? I have four social media platforms, three emails, two laptops and a phone that connects all of it. My children call that conservative. How would I survive without these vital tools, and what effect do gadgets have on our sense of hope and purpose? Is it possible to leave the modern world and do what many of us only dream of: unplug?

I estimated it would take over $1,500 in airfare alone to interview Ken Deardorff. Ken lives in a remote section of Alaska, almost completely sheltered from the instant world we live in. He does not have a cellphone or social media accounts, and as far as internet goes, his bandwidth does not support video. I have never spoken with Deardorff. To communicate with him, my only options are to email him or visit. Many have toyed with the notion of unplugging from the fast-paced world. In 1973, Deardorff did.

As a veteran of Vietnam, Ken Deardorff was looking for the last frontier. He had read Leland Stowe's novel, <u>Crusoe of Lone-</u>

some Lake. *Stowe's book chronicles the successful homesteading efforts of Canadian, Ralph Edwards, and his isolated effort to tame a 160-acre plot of land on an unnamed lake in British Columbia. Deardorff was inspired to find that frontier—that line dividing civilization and the wild. After four million American citizens had filed claims under the Homestead Act, Deardorff would be the final person in American history to mail in a claim before the opportunity for free land was repealed in 1976. Deardorff's ownership papers for his homestead would not show up in the mail until 1988. Perhaps the Homestead Act did not want to let go of a widespread tradition of hard work on the frontier.*

I first read about Deardorff in 2010, when my daughter and I stopped at the Homestead National Monument, located in southeastern Nebraska. The first homesteaders in American history claimed the land that the park sits on. Deardorff's story and his 1945 Allis-Chalmers tractor are housed at the Heritage Center. Interviewing Ken Deardorff is not simple, since he has no phone and weak Wi-Fi. I took a gamble and tried something new. With Deardorff in agreement, I emailed him one question at a time, and as the answers unfolded, I asked a few follow up questions. The obstacle of communication was overcome, and as a result, this new way of interviewing will benefit many people. Deardorff is private, but he offered a glimpse into his life and mindset as an Alaskan homesteader and its effect on his discovery of hope and purpose. He is highly reflective and this style of interview, by his own insight, enhanced his answers.

Overcoming the obstacles of cutting and plowing virgin Alaskan forest, almost independently, presents its daily challenges. Homesteading creates countless mental and physical daily encounters. Why do it? Does overcoming hurdles have a relationship with the rediscovery of hope and purpose, and if so, how do we dig deep within ourselves to find a mindset of how to take on challenges as a natural pattern within our daily lives? Does unplugging from a fast-paced world allow for the rediscovery of hope and purpose? Those were the overarching questions that swirled in my mind before I interviewed Deardorff.

ALBRECHT: I spoke to Mark Engler, the Superintendent of Homestead, if he felt it would be OK for me to reach out to you to be interviewed by phone. He must have emailed you, because he came back and said that you do not have a phone. I laughed at this because Mark has two cellphones clipped to his belt. You even each other out! Would you consider doing an interview with me, perhaps over the computer? Thank you for considering my request.

DEARDORFF: Sure. I would be available to answer whatever questions I am able. It will need to be in a Q & A format in text as our internet connection is too slow to support a video or Skype type of interface. If you would like to just send a list of questions, I will attempt to address them individually. If this won't work for you, I understand. It sounds like a worthwhile effort.

ALBRECHT: How would you define yourself?

DEARDORFF: Wow, that's a very broad question, so I will use very general terms. Sociable but not social. Maybe a bit aloof but I can "play the game" when it is appropriate. Pragmatic...but with a streak of pessimism. I like to think of it as realistic. I can do better with greater specificity.

ALBRECHT: You will see that the questions I ask are broad. It is a tough question because not many people ever ask questions like this.

DEARDORFF: You're correct. It isn't something people normally ask of themselves or others. I don't feel the need to define my-

self relative to others. I feel pretty much self-contained and confident. Hubris??? Maybe. But it works.

ALBRECHT: How do you define hope?

DEARDORFF: Hope is a vision of a future that could be better than
the present. It is something to be visualized in the mind's eye but
also something to keep a tight rein on. In my opinion, too many
people think HOPE is a viable strategy for navigating life. It isn't. It
can be a motivating force as long as the vision is realistic.

ALBRECHT: You live in Alaska. My understanding is that you grew
up in California. What events unfolded that brought you to homesteading in Alaska?

DEARDORFF: I don't recall any specific event that made me want
to go to Alaska. But I do remember by age five or six absolutely hating California, especially the weather, the crowding, and
the prevalent attitude in the country that California represented
something admirable and desirable. Remember, this was the early 50s, and I suspect that the memories of the Dust Bowl were still
strong. That Manifest Destiny still had some pull on the nation as
a whole, and that HOPE for something better was a ubiquitous
characteristic. But, for me, there were already too many people.
The weather was 'uncivilized'. Anywhere it can be ninety-five degrees on Christmas isn't fit for human habitation.

The attitude that people could change the direction of their
lives simply by changing location was prevalent and, to me, short
sighted. I was not very patient with that attitude, or those who
held it. It seemed to me that group think held sway in California.
As a teacher you may be familiar with the Turner thesis: that the
frontier in America was closed circa 1900. That felt very restric-
tive to me, and I didn't want to accept it. Alaska seemed to be the
antithesis to Turner, and it was a lot cooler, cleaner, less overrun

with people, and brimming with opportunity if one was willing to take some reasonable risk.

If there was one seminal event in fixing my course north, it was reading the book, <u>Crusoe of Lonesome Lake</u>—the story of Ralph Edwards near Bella Coola, British Columbia, at the turn of the 20th century. I think I was around eight to ten years old when I read the book. I still have a copy somewhere.

ALBRECHT: In Alaska, I would guess (though I have never been there... but, someday I will visit), there are many obstacles different than those that people have in the lower 48 states. As you see it, what type of mindset is necessary to overcome obstacles that face us on a daily basis? Or, on a once in a lifetime basis?

DEARDORFF: I don't think I would go that far. Urban Alaska is really not much different from urban California or any other stateside city. We have a saying up here that *the nice thing about Anchorage is that it is so close to Alaska. Fairbanks is a bit closer to the 'old Alaska'*. But all in all, I think the pressures on people are very similar in urban areas regardless of where they are located. Get out in *bush Alaska*, and you are talking about something entirely different.

Can you picture the angst in urban dwellers in general if they couldn't order a pizza for delivery, had no internet connection for days or weeks at a time, no cell service, not much in the way of groceries at the store, if there is one, mail delivery once or twice a week or not at all, ten dollar per gallon gasoline, electricity at 70 cents per kilowatts, sporadic access to health care, and lack of law enforcement. Here's a little trivia: the Alaska State Trooper who lives across the road from me is responsible for an area the size of Washington state and Oregon combined. How about no road access? Weather permitting, you might be able to get to a doctor appointment in "town", but the chances are just as good that there won't be a flight due to bad weather.

Now those things are all inconveniences for sure, but they are also a choice. Many of us view the trade off as worth it.

Anyway, you asked what type of mindset is necessary—In another-than-urban setting, I think the old cliché applies: *Any man who needs to ask for help, shouldn't start out in the first place.*

I want to add a corollary of sorts to my cliché: *Take little bites.* In other words, set reasonable goals for each day. Don't try to accomplish everything at once. That is a recipe for disappointment. Take on a small part of a large project each day and accomplish that. It gives a sense of success. It also prevents being mentally overwhelmed by the magnitude of the whole. It lets a person concentrate on doing each part of the task as well as possible. If you can do that, the complete project will turn out much better. Maybe not perfect, but pretty close.

ALBRECHT: I have never interviewed a person over email, but this is working. Another person interviewed in the book is Kathrine Switzer. She was the first female who illegally ran in the Boston Marathon—no women until 1972—she ran in '68. She reminded me that suffrage was closer to that race than it is to today. Your answer reflects what a short time ago the Dust Bowl and the sentiments of Manifest Destiny were holding on. However, the people who are witnesses to those events are slowly going, and therefore it seems quite distant.

DEARDORFF: Distant for sure, and well worth gathering and saving. It reminds me of the movie, "Leadbelly". Still today, we benefit from one of FDR's programs, while still suffering from the idea behind them generally. That program involved people being sent out to gather music, oral traditions, recipes, folktales, etc. Make work for sure, but in the case of Leadbelly, we have a record of his music as well as a social commentary on the times he lived through. Alan Lomax compiled a great volume of traditional music through this program, and Leadbelly was one of his interviewees. Being a half-assed musician, I appreciate that effort. It was worth it.

I think the email method is superior because it allows time for thought rather than expediency.

ALBRECHT: I do work and collaborate with the Smithsonian Folklife and Center for Cultural Heritage. They do a lot of recording and preservation of culture and daily life around the world. It creates a peaceful median for diverse interactions.

DEARDORFF: That makes me remember a visit to the John C. Campbell Folk School in North Carolina. A delightful place to learn new things and rest your soul at the same time.

Well, as you might suspect, alleviating heavy labor was a huge motivator. I knew that I needed several large, heavy logs to build a permanent house. How was I to move them? All I had was my body and eventually a mechanical come along (this was prior to the tractor). Through trial and error, I figured out I needed to clear a path to drag the logs to the river so they could be floated to where I needed them. But the darn things snagged on every root and bush nearby. Finally, I remembered a photo I had seen in a book on early logging in the Pacific northwest. I eventually made a trough of sorts out of smaller poles that could be used as a skid road. That really helped, but it wasn't quite all I needed. I knew that I had to remove the bark from the logs so they would dry, but I wanted to keep them as clean as possible until I got them in place. Nevertheless, I peeled one in the woods and started dragging it. WHAT A DIFFERENCE!!! There is a fluid between the bark and the cambium layer of the tree that provides lubrication. Now the logs slid, not easily, but with much less effort than previously. The lesson was that even though it took me a lot of days to construct my skid road, it saved many days and my back in the long run. TAKE LITTLE BITES!

Food preservation: It's easy in the winter to keep food safe in rural Alaska. But, what to do in the summer when you have no refrigeration? One solution is to dry fish and meat. That works, but it is labor intensive, so the second spring I was on the homestead I was raking up sawdust from an area where I had cut wood the previous winter. I wanted the spot for a garden. Under the sawdust, I found ice. The light comes on. Old technology rules in these situations. Long story shortened, I built a small log icehouse and all during the next winter I filled it with ice blocks cut from the river and covered them with sawdust from cutting firewood. This accomplished three things in one project. It provided cold storage for leftovers, etc. during summer months, it kept the sawdust cleared off my garden area, and it allowed me to reduce my efforts at fishing for food since I was now able to utilize more of what I gathered rather than see it go to waste. That allowed me to spend more time on other jobs.

To this day I try to combine tasks. If I have an object or tool that needs to go to my shop, I will wait to take it there until I also need to get something else from that location. There is ALWAYS more work to do, so never go either direction with your hands empty.

Clearing land: On the homestead I was required to remove the stumps of trees I had cut down. I tried digging them out, but that took several days of backbreaking toil. I had no tractor or bulldozer at this time. The stumps were about twenty-four inches in diameter with complex root systems. I could see I was never going to succeed at this rate.

I thought maybe I could use some sort of explosives to remove them. How does a guy do that? I was about to make my annual trip to Anchorage to see my dentist and buy gear and supplies for the coming year. I ended up at the library. I found the Blaster's Handbook. I spent a couple of days reading and learning the basics. Next, I found an industrial supply store in Anchorage that sold dynamite. Remember, this was the early 1970s, when people still had a few liberties.

Anyway, I bought a couple hundred pounds of dynamite, fuses, caps, and a tool to crimp the caps onto the fuses. To say I felt confident would be an exaggeration. Just flying with the stuff worried me. The dynamite itself was pretty safe, but the caps (detonators) concerned me. I could just imagine setting off an explosion in the plane when the radio transmit button was depressed. Anyway, eventually I had to teach myself to put these different components together and how to efficiently and safely place the charges under those large stumps. ONE STEP AT A TIME! Obviously, everything worked out. It was a successful experiment and reinforced my attitude of TAKE LITTLE BITES. DON'T RUSH. I had to first learn what I didn't know. Then I had to find a way to overcome my deficiency of experience and knowledge. I convinced myself that if others can do this, so can I. In fact, I can probably do it better than some but at least as well as most.

Books, patience, confidence.

ALBRECHT: Books, patience, confidence. I agree. I see this as a teacher. We say that we need to be patient with kids, but we need to teach kids patience too. I find that many people want things to be easy and fast. There is little reward in that. It develops false hope. There is a lot of value in learning through trial and error and being patient with learning a little at a time. Many kids and adults are afraid to fail, but this is where great learning takes place. I see confidence as the willingness to try and the strength to fail. Would you agree?

DEARDORFF: Absolutely! Too many, in my opinion, believe the Constitution guarantees them freedom FROM, rather than freedom TO. Look how many successful businesspeople have failed a few times. That's an indicator that ideas that are good in theory but don't pan out, aren't really good ideas. But at the same time, bad ideas can lead to better ideas that do work to some degree.

I have an annoying habit when I am faced with some sort of problem. I whine. It drives all of my friends crazy, and I understand that because it sounds so negative. But I know why I am whining. HONESTY. It even takes a fairly standard form. I will look at something and say, *gee, if I only had a... or I wish I could do this...* It serves a purpose. It makes me run alternative scenarios through my head. Eventually, one would hope, I will hit on something that actually is possible and does in fact work. I have a special place that I use to think about problems like that—the shower. If I stand in a hot shower, I can let my brain drift, while my body is enjoying the comfort of hot water. I don't know why it works, but it has proven to be productive for me.

Yes, the whole thing of instant gratification is detrimental.

ALBRECHT: You have the shower. I like to run long distances to do the same thing. It is amazing how many things get clear on a run when there are no distractions. Do you see a connection between hope and the ability to overcome obstacles? If so, can you give some further examples from your experience on the homestead?

DEARDORFF: My immediate response is NO. But I will ramble a bit anyway.

There COULD be a learned but unconscious correlation between hope and the ability to overcome obstacles. I think it would require 1. several years of being optimistic and successful at moving toward your vision of the future and 2. a very perceptive person to recognize the relationship within his own personality.

When I try to dredge up memories of this type of thing from my past, they all entail life threatening situations. Those types of situations almost never allow time for the conscious mind to consider abstract concepts like hope. They probably do involve an unconscious consideration of a future, but only within the context of *do I have a future?* Generally, in those situations, direct action takes the place of any intellectual exercise.

ALBRECHT: As a teacher, I have learned to expect the unexpected. Your answer was something that I had not considered because I have never homesteaded. I do backcountry hike a lot and enjoy the way it simplifies my mind over days. I have brought two of my children up on weeklong hikes, and I would say these are the greatest moments of my life with them. What I am taking away from your response is that hope is built over a long time with a lot of work. However, the immediate situations where you must react cerebrally does not build hope. Would you agree? So, as a follow up to your answer, and a question that arises from your answer is whether life and death are daily thoughts on an Alaskan homestead?

DEARDORFF: There is no place better than the wilderness to clear your mind and refresh your soul. It is my church and the way I worship. Your kids will always remember those times with you.

"Hope is built over a long time with a lot of work". I would say, no. The hope is always there whether one realizes it or not. I would say 'success' is built over a long time with a lot of work. And whether we are aware of it or not those successes are cumulative in achieving our vision (hope).

Life and death—yes, I would say it is always in the back of

one's mind. It was no doubt the same on farms in the 19th and 20th century and probably still is. It isn't something that a guy thinks about but it is something that alters behavior in a subtle way, every day. Safety becomes a state of mind because there is no one to rely on except yourself. When I originally mentioned "life and death" I was thinking of things that are common here: wild animals, drowning, broken bones, or other injuries or illnesses a person might experience. I was also thinking about Vietnam. You can spend all the time in the world wishing and hoping that those things don't happen, but a lot of that is within your control. So, caution becomes second nature. For example, let's say I need to set a net in the river to catch salmon. I put my gear in the boat and am ready to leave the bank. Do I go upstream or downstream? The correct or the BEST answer is UPSTREAM. If I have an engine problem or injure myself, I can at least drift downstream to get home. If I am downstream and possibly on the opposite side, how do I get home? What about my family back at the cabin? Anyway, you get the idea. Just simple things that need to be considered. Hope won't help if you make dumb choices.

ALBRECHT: Do you have a code that you live by? Or, if you could convey one message about how to live to every person, what would it be?

DEARDORFF: I do. I even have a small wooden box that I keep small, meaningful items inside. It has a brass plate on the lid with the following engraved. The meaning, to me, is all-encompassing: *Victory with Honor.*

ALBRECHT: Do you have a favorite teacher? If so, who is he or she? Where did that person teach you?

DEARDORFF: Oh, that's an easy one! Yes, I did. His name was NB Martin. He taught at the College of the Sequoias, a small two-year school I attended after the army. I took classes in US history, Latin-American history, and European history from him. Most students disliked him intensely and avoided his classes. He was a serious person who knew his subject. He had no patience for unserious students. His classes were difficult, but I loved them. He expected performance. He also expected the student to work as hard as he did. This is not to say he was unkind or unhelpful. He wasn't. Get him in his office, and he was sociable and easy-going. He was a WW2 fighter pilot in the Pacific and an any-ocean, any-tonnage master mariner—one heck of an interesting guy. I did develop a bad habit from him. I, too, expect as much from others as I do from myself. I have been disappointed many, many times. On the other hand, over the years I have had occasion to hire a few people to work with or for me. I sort of modified my expectations. I decided that it is unreasonable to expect that everyone has the same tools and knowledge available to them. I also decided it is best to explain EXACTLY what you want AND how to achieve that if the other person needs direction. It is my responsibility to help them meet my expectations. Once you have done that, get out of the way and let them do it. I believe that if you give people responsibility for doing something, they will more often than not be successful. They have to know you trust them and have confidence in them. In other words, they need to know you have high expectations of them, and you are confident they can achieve it.

NB Martin, I am sure, influenced that thinking. He also activated in me a behavior that I call "Academic Darwinism." All through college I had a ruthless attitude toward the other students in my classes. I was going to be the best in any particular class, so do your best or stay out of the way, especially in classes where the professor graded on a curve. It wasn't an effort to harm others but rather a device I used to push myself. Anyway, I hope you can see the influence NB Martin had on me in many aspects of my life since that time.

ALBRECHT: Thank you for sharing all your thoughts and experiences. It has been a pleasure.

Deardorff's interview will spark a lot of thought, but there is a reason he moved to Alaska. His strength and joy are built around the environment he has chosen. I was fortunate to correspond with him because of our overlapping interest in homesteading. He prefers a life of reflection without interruptions. It is important to respect his way of life by remembering to not reach out to him to allow him that peace. Thank you for respecting that.

- 2 -

GEORGE WASHINGTON CARVER, like Ken Deardorff, was a homesteader. His numerous discoveries and inventions include adhesives, axel grease, buttermilk, fire briquettes, linoleum, meat tenderizer, bleach, instant coffee, shaving cream, shoe polish, and wood stain, among many others. Countless products that we enjoy today can be credited to him. He developed three hundred uses for peanuts and hundreds more for soybeans, pecans, and sweet potatoes. Carver did not patent or profit from most of his products; he lived by the belief that giving freely to mankind outweighed personal gain. Despite all of his work, only three patents were issued to him during his lifetime. Upon his death, he had a mere $60,000 in savings, all of which was donated to the establishment of the Carver Research Foundation at Tuskegee University to provide for continued research in agriculture. Carver was a professor there for forty-three years.

George Washington Carver's notoriety is coupled with an unusual start. Carver was born into slavery on an unknown day on a plantation in Diamond, Missouri. His master, Moses Carver, was a German American immigrant, who had purchased George's parents, Mary and Giles, on October 9th, 1855, for $700. As an infant, he, a sister, and his mother were kidnapped at night by thieves from Arkansas. Moses Carver hired a man named John Bentley to locate and return them, but he found only the infant, George. Once slavery was abolished, Moses Carver and his wife, Susan, raised George and his older brother, James, as their own children. They encouraged George to continue his intellectual pursuits, and "Aunt Susan" taught him the basics of reading and writing because black people were not allowed at the public school in Diamond Grove. Carver would walk ten miles to attend a school designated for black children. Freedom and citizenship came early in Carver's life, but opportunities did not.

Carver met Mariah Watkins, a citizen of Neosho, while he was attending school. He wished to rent a room. When he identified himself as "Carver's George," as he had done his whole life, she countered that from now on his name was "George Carver." An impressionable young George Carver was told, "You must learn all you can, then go back out into the world and give your learning back to the people." Watkins's advice had a lasting impact on Carver's approach to life. Racial divide challenged Carver's pursuits, but the discovery of hope and purpose is paved with potholes and hills to climb. Numerous institutions of higher education turned his requests for admission down, so Carver turned to homesteading, and with proven practical success, became the first person of color to be admitted to Iowa State University.

In 1896, Booker T. Washington, the first principal and president of the Tuskegee Institute, presented Carver with the opportunity to head its Agriculture Department. Working off of a homesteader's practical mindset, he took what he had observed

and educated students on the benefits of crop rotation and experimentation, agricultural practices that improved soil quality in
areas that were depleted by years of farming cotton, and taught
generations of black students farming techniques for self-suf-
ficiency. Upon his death, Carver was buried next to Booker T.
Washington in a simple grave that reads: *He could have added
fortune to fame, but caring for neither, he found happiness and
honor in being helpful to the world.*

What would a world of no obstacles look like? Obstacles create growth, and hope and purpose emerge as challenges are conquered. The human soul yearns to achieve something. However,
by nature and early nurturing, the obstacles a person wishes to
tackle can be as unique as fingerprints, and it is up to each individual whether they are going to take on the obstacles or let
them crush their identity.

Ken Deardorff and George Washington Carver not only were
successful homesteaders, but they also lived similar lives. Whether it is the connection to homesteading, the pursuit of education, or the points at which they lived, Deardorff and Carver's
individual aspirations defined them. Carver and Deardorff both
possessed original thought, resourcefulness, and crafted systems
that worked in the environments that they were surviving in. All
are key components that provide a guidebook to the development of hope.

Before I communicated with Ken Deardorff, I had assumptions.
I wanted Ken to confirm that hard work led to the discovery of
hope and purpose. I was convinced that hard work on a homestead would lead to a level of hope. He shifted my thinking. He
explained that hard work may lead to success, but hope is always
present. This is a profound turning point in the rediscovery of

hope. If, as Deardorff explains, hope is always present within us, we are all capable of discovering what is already there. How is that tapped into? Deardorff lit a crystal-clear path, and it sheds light on the life decisions of George Washington Carver.

When Deardorff chose to leave California after returning from Vietnam, he selected Alaska and homesteading. Under the Homestead Act, Deardorff was pursuing a goal—if he lived on and farmed his homestead, he would gain free land. The challenges that came with this endeavor were nearly infinite and could not always be anticipated. By Deardorff's own admission, his most challenging obstacles did not build hope. He was in a mode of survival, and some situations required quick thinking, not hoping. Deardorff is quick to point out that hope can be a motivating force if the vision is realistic. How many people do you know that are too busy, overworked, and not living a simple life? The complexity of a fast-paced world has caused people of all ages to set goals that are lofty. The result is an inability to be satisfied with a reasonable goal that is healthy. By setting simple goals, the pressure of taking work home disappears; it allows people to live in the mindset of *taking little bites.* By breaking down work into small chunks, people are able to make steady progress instead of constantly racing against the clock.

In baseball, there is one word all batters dread: slump. Baseball is a parallel to life. Slumps happen, but what a person does with a slump will determine his future. Even in moments of failure, frustration, and anger, every person has a choice of how to direct their mindset. Survivors do what Deardorff suggests and are *realistic.* As a teacher, I continually cringe when I hear high schools across the United States incorporate *career and college ready* in their mission statements. I would hope that no person on their deathbed says that their greatest accomplishment was their career or their college. Rather, an educational institution should stop forcing young minds into spaces they do not belong and allow people more flexibility to explore their dreams. Realistically, each person must earn a living to put food on the table and a roof over their family's head, but I urge schools to teach balance. People need time to explore what they would want to talk about in their last hours of life. This ensures a balance of realistic work and happiness.

Realism plays into Ken Deardorff's understanding of hope. In his words: "Hope is a vision of a future that could be better than the present. It is something to be visualized in the mind's eye. It can be a motivating force as long as the vision is realistic." The recognition that hope is in the present and easily attainable is a validating notion if a person decides to be grounded in realism. For Deardorff, the rediscovery of hope and purpose begins with simplification. Remove the unnecessary clutter in your life and the clouds will clear to show the rays of hope. The challenge is making the decision of what to remove. In a materialistic world where all things seem consumable and attainable, we must be able to say, *enough is enough.* Gratification is as easy as a key stroke on a computer, but is this addiction a want or a need? If it is not a need, and you cannot walk away from it, it is a cluttering addiction. Deardorff confirmed that struggles often outweigh conveniences when he said, "now those things are all inconveniences for sure, but they are also a choice. Many of us view the trade off as worth it."

Honesty holds a golden key to understanding hope and purpose. Switching careers, changing hairstyles, or taking up yoga will not change a person's situation. That attitude was held by many Alaskan homesteaders of Deardorff's era. Simply deciding to do something new only defines actions, not attitudes. Actions are short lived, but a total change of mindset can create life-altering shifts. The goal to simplify life does not mean replacing, though it may mean forcing the removal of something significant. Depending on circumstances, the pursuit of hope may be the most difficult decision a person has to make to build a life of fulfillment. Hope takes grit. Deardorff said it best when he stated, "Simple things that need to be considered. Hope will not help if you make dumb choices."

Though the pursuit of simplification seems paradoxical because of all the work that must be done, it does not all have to be done at the same time. The goal is to make tomorrow better than today and repeat that action every day. Instead of trying to finish everything at once, try to take small steps to accomplish more modest goals. People who rush though meaningful events are only creating a recipe for disappointment. Amazing accomplishments do not have to start with an amazing first step. I am sure that there was nothing noteworthy about Sir Edmund Hilary's first step on his pioneering ascent of Mt. Everest. He most likely looked ahead and simply put one foot in front of the other. Had he started in a mad sprint, not only would it have been comical, but he never would have been the first to scale the great mountain. Realistic expectations of those around us need to be embraced, or imbalance develops. If "I" am entitled to simplification, then "we" are too.

Though there are basics that all people need to know, we need to teach children right from birth about patience and the importance of continous self-education. In an analogy to the Alaskan wilderness, Deardorff said that "any man who needs to ask for help, shouldn't start out in the first place." That does not mean that a person is forever prevented from fulfilling their dreams.

It just means that once a person simplifies their life and identifies their priorities, self-education is necessary to become truly independent. The right books, combined with patience, lead to confidence.

In 1893, Frederick Jackson Turner presented the frontier thesis—also known as the Turner thesis. For years, Turner argued that American culture was unique because of the presence of a frontier line that kept expanding west for the first 120 years of the country's existence. The frontier line separates cultivated soil from that of the wilderness. When Deardorff referenced the Turner thesis, I realized I had not heard the term since my junior year of college. It is a term that goes back to a period when there was still land to be explored as America expanded westward. Once the west coast had been reached in the late 1800s, the frontier was essentially closed. However, there was still Alaska. Finding the frontier is not for everyone, but it was perfect for Deardorff. The rediscovery of hope and purpose involves the most basic of human desires—the pursuit of happiness and the fulfillment of dreams. For Deardorff, it was crucial to disprove Turner by finding that magical trail that stretches towards the untouched wilderness. For hope to flourish, all people need to unleash dreams before time takes away the ability to pursue those dreams, and it is each person's responsibility to support others in that pursuit. As Deardorff put it, in the end:

> There COULD be a learned, but unconscious correlation between hope and the ability to overcome obstacles. I think it would require several years of being optimistic and successful at moving toward your vision of the future and a very perceptive person to recognize the relationship within his own personality. The hope

is always there whether one realizes it or not. I would
say 'success' is built over a long time with a lot of work.
And, whether we are aware of it or not, those successes
are cumulative in achieving our vision (hope).

- 3 -

A PERSON WHO has never failed is a person who has never taken a risk. Those that do not take at least some risk in their life, even in defense of their own thoughts, has lost sight of their hope and purpose. When I fail, I go through a cycle. What could I have done differently? Is someone angry? Who did I let down? Failure is anything but fun, but neither was walking home from school when I was an adolescent. The bones in my feet were growing at all different rates, causing unbelievable pain. The doctors told me and my parents that it was normal. Apparently, there are more bones in a person's foot than there are anywhere else in the body. Some bones decide to grow before waiting for others to join, and the net result is painful feet, along with a whole host of other issues. Adolescence is one rite of passage that I feel God screwed up. However, eventually all those bones caught up, and my feet did not hurt again until I was in my late forties. Now it seems my night vision, knees, hips, and memory are a little off. Logic tells me to cross train, run less, and eat better. I need to follow a path to the fountain of youth through daily moderate exercise, limited alcohol, and better eating. Goodbye cheese pizza and macaroni salad with real mayonnaise.

I have been team teaching for twenty-two years with my partner, Mrs. Stoker. We met ten days after being hired and immediately had to begin working as a team. I took over English Language Arts and science, and she took over math and Social

Studies. We have a home base of about twenty-four students per class, but we share all forty-eight kids. When we met, I had one child, and she was Miss Maar. I now have three kids, and she is happily married to the band teacher with two boys. When we started, there were no grey hairs in sight, but now, we just try to convince ourselves that salt and pepper hair is in style. We plan to retire in the same year. That is a long way off and a lot could change, but our history together feels like it is etched in granite.

Have we argued? Of course, but not much after our first three years. It took a few years to learn about each other and what each of us values. Compromise is an art that takes years of patience to develop. Mrs. Stoker is fun, and I am strict; I loosened up, and she became more accountable. Did we ever make mistakes? Yes. There was one open house where we sent totally different messages about what is not important. We have both been frustrated—*really* frustrated—with each other, but we knew to let our heads cool for a bit so that we could talk it out.

What was compromise like? Honestly, it was not really the compromise that was a challenge. We would spend hours trying to figure out how to match our irregular schedules. We needed to be patient and listen to each other's ideas. What took us hours at the beginning of our careers is now a five-minute conversation; sometimes it feels like we are reading each other's mind. I am sure in our first years we both considered moving on. Instead, we worked on our team. It was not easy, but after getting into a pattern that results in the best education we can give our students, all that hard work has given both of us happiness, which provides us with hope and purpose.

Failure is not the end; rather, failure is life's best opportunity to grow. Failure itself is not the problem. It is the way that individuals react to failure that makes all the difference in the world. Mrs.

Stoker and I are a perfect case study. Both of us have screwed up, and there is no doubt in my mind that I have made more mistakes than her. I tend to take more chances. There are some essential steps that need to take place when failure happens. Failure is a fork in the road. It can lead to anger, guilt, divorce, and can destroy perseverance, growth, and hope if it is handled poorly. I am fortunate to have a partner that shares a common understanding.

There is no doubt that at some point each of us will embarrass ourselves, and make the people around us question, "Why am I here?" Failure exposes our vulnerability, faith, and hope, and if handled poorly, is one of the considerable obstacles in the face of the development of hope and purpose. Hope and purpose are two of the most difficult identities we must build as partners, humans, and individuals. Their development helps us acknowledge the fact that we have all failed at something. The way we react to personal, partner, and team failures defines if we are able to develop hope and purpose. Reactions such as talking behind a person's back, not treating your partner as your equal, or failing to understand forgiveness will stop growth in its tracks. Growth is hope's cousin.

With all of that said, Mrs. Stoker and I are not perfect. We fail each other but never on purpose. We recognize that each of our humanity is no different than the other's. In the end, I will feel lucky if we can retire together. If this happens, we will have enjoyed thirty-two years teaching alongside of each other. We only get one life, and if Mrs. Stoker and I live to see a century, we will have shared over thirty percent of our lives working together. I ask this—why is that rare? If I am being completely honest, I am proud to have failed; I chose to grow from it.

I have learned a lot from Mrs. Stoker. Most of all—listen to a person who has something constructive to say and be open to changing direction based on his feedback. This is easily said, but it takes some grit to get it done.

One of the challenges of the discovery of hope is that sometimes the harder you search for it, the more disguised it becomes. A person's purpose in life is not tied to a timeline. Some people find their purpose early in life, while others may need more time to discover themselves. Spike Lee gave Samuel L. Jackson his first break as an actor at forty-three, Julia Child released her first cookbook at age fifty, and my personal favorite, the legend of college cuisine, Momofuku Ando, invented instant noodles at age fifty. The list goes on. Vera Wang trained her whole life to become a figure skater. She did not make it to the Olympics and became a fashion designer at age forty. Ray Kroc incorporated McDonalds at age fifty-two, and Stan Lee, regarded as the greatest comic book artist of all time, published his first work at thirty-nine. His creations include Spiderman, the Fantastic Four, the Black Panther, and the X-Men. Hope is timeless and ageless. Purpose is for all people, except those that are dead.

Harland Sanders was a jack of all trades. He bounced from job to job in Kentucky searching for his purpose in life. When my mother was alive, she often reminded me that life starts at forty. I do not think Sanders would disagree with Mom's wisdom. When Sanders was forty, the Great Depression was in its first year. He was a fireman, insurance salesman, and gas station owner. At one point, he owned a hotel, but it burned to the ground. He rebuilt it only to see World War II deliver a crushing blow on the tourism industry. However, Sanders created a great restaurant in that hotel. You might be familiar with the specialty: Kentucky Fried Chicken. People loved it to the point that food critic, Dunkin Hines, visited his restaurant. At this point, Colonel Harland Sanders was nearly sixty years old. The title "Colonel" came arbitrarily from his good friend, Kentucky Governor Lawrence "Happy" Wetherby. At age sixty-two, Harland Sanders, now known as Colonel Sanders, sold his first franchise to Pete Harman of South Salt Lake, Utah. Kentucky Fried Chicken became an instant hit in the heart of Mormon country. In his first year as a franchisee, Harman saw a seventy-five percent increase in food sales, all due to the secret fried chicken recipe. Even with the progress in Utah, success was slow growing. Just as his local restaurant was gaining some traction, the construction of a nearby highway put him out of business. He then made over 1,000 pitches of his chicken recipe to investors before, at age sixty-eight, his empire caught on.

At the time of Colonel Sanders's death in 1980, there were over 6,000 Kentucky Fried Chicken franchised restaurants worldwide. For the final twenty years of his life, Colonel Sanders only wore a heavy wool suit in the winter and a light cotton suit in the summer, all white with his trademark ribbon tie. He even bleached his mustache and goatee to match his white hair.

Have you looked in the mirror lately? Have you seen wrinkles, a drop in your 401K, or are you just frustrated that age is taking your life away? At some point a person's body and mind are just not what they were in their prime. It would be a lie to say otherwise. However, a man selling fried chicken at nearly seventy years old found his hope and purpose in life. So, what if it came later in life? The important thing is that Colonel Harlan Sanders did not die hopeless. Hope and purpose come to those that never stop trying and do not rely on others to pick them up. People with hope and purpose discover it for themselves. Look in the mirror. Do you still have a dream or hope? It is never too late to start to find your purpose in life.

Chapter 6
Keep Your Brain Open for Business

"I think that hope is something that you survive on as much as food, water and shelter."

-Peter Mehlman

- 1 -

Each May, I send an invitation to my former students that are finishing their senior year of high school. Every fourth-grade student has to bring in a leftover toilet paper roll. After a few weeks of writing, revising, and editing, they fold a letter from their fourth-grade self to their graduating self. There are few limits as to what the students can write about; I encourage them to write about childhood crushes, secrets, and their most intimate thoughts. I do not read the letters, and they are stuffed in that repurposed brown tube, capped, and kept hidden from the light of day for eight years. A few weeks prior to graduation, the students are invited to meet and open their letters. The awkwardness of the reunion is compounded by their nine-year-old voice revealing their innermost thoughts. The honesty of a nine-year-old is comical, especially when that honesty is turned towards what they think will be most important to their near-adult selves. Their awkwardness is almost universally followed by laughter. People that make us laugh have a huge impact on our happiness. What effect does laughter have on the rediscovery of hope and purpose?

Peter Mehlman started a career with The Washington Post in sports journalism in the late 1970s. In 1982, his career shifted to television as a writer for Howard Cosell's Sports Beat. With absolutely no experience in script writing, in 1989 he was offered a position by producer Larry David to write a freelance script for the new television sitcom, Seinfeld. Mehlman submitted a short humorous piece he wrote for The New York Times Magazine. Comedian, Jerry Seinfeld, saw Mehlman's talent instantly and brought him to California, where he freelance wrote the episode titled, "The Apartment." Mehlman was hired in 1991 for the first full season of Seinfeld as a program consultant. Six years later, he would reach the level of co-executive producer.

Seinfeld is arguably the most successful comedy in television history. With audience sizes in the hundreds of millions of viewers, the one-liners and hilarious hijinks have reached iconic status. A major force behind their creation is Peter Mehlman. Mehlman brought to life phrases such as 'double dipping,' 'yada, yada, yada,' 'Get Out!,' 'shrinkage,' and 'sponge worthy.' Mehlman wrote or co-wrote twenty-two Seinfeld episodes. Does the discovery of hope and purpose have a connection to comedy? Is creativity an important ingredient for their development? Peter Mehlman is an expert on both questions.

ALBRECHT: I appreciate you taking the time to talk with me. I found a connection between us. I saw an interview you were part of a few years back. You spoke about little things that are humorous sticking in your brain. That happens to me too. First off, you have led an interesting life. How would you define yourself?

MEHLMAN: Ummm, um, um, um... you know, I think that I am just an observer. If I had to put it down to one word, I would just say, *I'm an observer.* That's kind of what drew me to journalism and then into comedy as well. Even though I wasn't a very serious student in high school and college, I was a learner. I just try to observe and learn all the time. When I first did *Seinfeld*, I had never written scripts before. I was a little in over my head, and about two weeks in, you know, just sitting in meetings and talking to the other people, seeing the way showbusiness works, and everything like that, which was all new to me, I wrote down on this piece of paper this little phrase—*Shut up and learn.* I think that is the best advice I ever gave myself. I think if I had to have a motto for my life, that would be it.

ALBRECHT: Shut up and learn?

MEHLMAN: Shut up and learn.

ALBRECHT: Prior to *Seinfeld*, you were working with Howard Cosell. I was surprised to read that you went from your work with Cosell to *Seinfeld*.

MEHLMAN: Yeah, they seem largely at odds with each other, but you know, from someone like Howard Cosell, there was so much to learn. I was a sports guy, and before that I had written sports for *The Washington Post*. I was such a sports nut, by the time I was involved in it professionally, like at the *Post*—I will never forget the first time I covered a Baltimore Orioles game, and I was interviewing Jim Palmer, and I felt weirdly embarrassed asking this seemingly really bright guy about *what were you thinking when you threw that pitch?* All of the sudden it seemed all so pointless and dopey, and somehow, I wound up with Howard Cosell. His whole view of sports was that you've gotta not separate sports from the real world. This goes beyond just sitting, mindlessly watching games. In certain ways, Howard really tainted my view of sports and somewhat compromised my enjoyment of sports. But, at the same time I think it is important to have a realistic view of things. Cosell always talked about the *jockocracy* and the sports syndrome where nothing matters but winning and all that. I just can't see it that way.

I'm still happy that certain athletes catch my attention, and I get a little rooting interest. I felt that way, like the first time I saw

Kobe Bryant play. I don't know why. I was just kind of transfixed. I was a huge, huge Kobe Bryant fan. I really followed him. I think part of it is like Howard preached, you've got to kind of humanize sports. To blindly root for a team just because they're the Yankees just started seeming nuts to me. I was a lifelong Yankee fan, but when they lost to the Red Sox in 2004, afterwards I remember thinking *if I weren't a Yankee fan, and I looked at those two teams, I probably would have rooted for the Red Sox.* The guys on the team were funnier and more interesting. I loved Derek Jeter, but he never said anything really interesting.

I did a whole bunch of sports interviews called *Peter Mehlman's Narrow World of Sports.* I got to interview Kobe, Tiger Woods, and Blade Griffen, and I asked them the questions that I wanted to ask. It was kind of a reaction against ESPN and all the dumb jock bland questions they ask. They knew I was from a comedy background, so they knew it was all about comedy. We all get tired of athletes spinning their clichés like *one game at a time, I just want to contribute,* and *it was a total team effort.* Nobody jumps on the sports media people who ask questions that are no less bland than that.

ALBRECHT: Were you a trained writer to start out with? Was this something that you loved as a kid? Were you always writing?

MEHLMAN: No, not that I was aware of. Somehow in college I gravitated over to the newspaper office. The University of Maryland actually had one of the best student newspapers in the country. I don't know why. I just gravitated over there and ended up writing articles. Then, I was also naturally drawn to certain writers, and I didn't know why. They were recommended. I started reading Philip Roth, and I read an interview with him, and he said *John Updike is the best writer in America.* Then I became really into Updike. Then on to Joan Didion and all these other writers. I started seeing that having your own writing voice is really important and, you know, you mentioned the word *goals...* you know, I've never had any goals. I'm not a really big believer in goals. To me, why limit yourself?

ALBRECHT: Well, that is consistent with being an observer, I think. An observer takes what's around them and captures it.

MEHLMAN: You never know where one thing is going to lead you, especially in this business. You write one thing, and the right person or the wrong person reads it, and you can be off on a whole new avenue of life. I got hired to *Seinfeld* on the basis of an article in *The New York Times*. Jerry and Larry were looking for writers and were asking for writing samples. Everyone was turning in scripts. I am turning in an essay from *The New York Times*. Luckily, Larry and Jerry didn't know what they were doing as far as running a sitcom, so they were taken more by what I wrote than a spec-script for *Who's the Boss?*.

ALBRECHT: So, you went toward *Seinfeld*. Before we talk about *Seinfeld*, how would you define hope?

MEHLMAN: I think that hope is something that you survive on as much as food, water, and shelter. You know, if you have some hope, for whatever you are hoping for, then you know, you will carry on. Hope is right up there with luck. Hope and luck are the two things that feed your life.

ALBRECHT: I see a lot of our current problems blamed on poverty, challenges, this circumstance and that circumstance, but I have come to the conclusion that a dry well of hope is more catastrophic. So, let's melt two things together. You were talking about the show *Seinfeld*. Does comedy and laughter have a connection to the development of hope? *Seinfeld* was a comedy about best friends consistently destroying each other. Even in this arena, do you see a connection between hope and laughter?

MEHLMAN: Absolutely! First of all, with *Seinfeld,* the feeling that a viewer gets that he or she is not alone in these completely off-beat thoughts that they might have. It's got to be very comforting. Laughter gives a little hope to people, so they understand that *I'm really not that weird.* These people on the show are think-ing the same thing that I am. That's what the show was about, and in a way, the most difficult transition for me because as an observer and in journalism, I was always kind of looking out at the world and observing. On *Seinfeld,* it was more about looking inward at yourself, capturing the small thoughts that you have, and then blowing them up in a script. The real original concepts of the show stories were very small, and they were based on tiny slices of life. That is the philosophy that I held onto for the run of the show. Even though, when the show got so popular and the money basically became unlimited, the stories got a little bit less realistic and became grander and more outlandish. Like, I really didn't want to write about really big episodes. I didn't want to write about a Puerto Rican Day parade. I just wanted to stick to the most basic human elements.

ALBRECHT: Can money then get in the way? Did money change the approach to the show?

MEHLMAN: I think to a certain degree, yes. You know, in the last couple of seasons I actually had to think about the last couple of sets that we had to put up. Any time you put up a new set on your stage it costs thousands and thousands of dollars, so I had to find ways to take the sets that we already had all the time that didn't cost anything new to put up and work within that as opposed to saying *Oh, I have all of the money in the world to play with. We could build a better bathroom set for this thirty-second scene.* We did that later on, but I kind of liked it more—I always liked having boundaries to push against. I liked having boundaries more than just complete freedom. There is in me a preference to write for *The New York Times* rather than *Rolling Stone* where you can say anything. Larry David was amazing at that. He did a twenty-two minute episode about masturbation, and it wasn't offensive to anyone. Once you can get away with doing a tactful twenty-two minutes on masturbation, I think you can pretty much get away with anything. I don't want to be that type of writer that uses joke lines.

I kind of avoided the word joke the entire time. What you really strived for on *Seinfeld* was having just a normal piece of dialogue that wasn't a joke and yet would still get a huge laugh. When George was dating a girl that had a huge nose, she points out how many beautiful women there are in New York, and Cramer points out that *you're as pretty as any of them. You just need a nose job.* That's not a joke. It's just dialogue that gets a huge laugh. That's what I would strive for.

ALBRECHT: So, *Seinfeld* gets really big, how do you remain creative under a pressure cooker like that? Being creative on the spot is very difficult to achieve. How do you do that?

MEHLMAN: Being creative on the spot is really hard. That's one area of talent that some writers have and some writers don't. That wasn't exactly my strongpoint. The show got incredibly popular and all that. I just tried to think about the show at large and—my other kind of motto was just *keep your brain open for business*—look around, listen to the radio, watch TV, have a pad on you at all times and then write down thoughts. The whole thing was about creating some mechanism in your brain to where you're living your life, but you're also observing at the same time. You know, that's tough to balance sometimes.

ALBRECHT: That's very tough. It can become consuming.

MEHLMAN: Yeah, when it becomes consuming, that's when you have to back off. Just trust that you don't always have to be aware of your own thoughts. You can live your life and still be observant enough to catch what's going through your head.

ALBRECHT: So then, what makes you laugh the most?

MEHLMAN: [long pause] You know, what makes me laugh is not so much humor or outright funny things. What makes me laugh is wit. Fran Leibowitz makes me laugh because what she says is so witty and so perfectly worded and then a funny persona, Sarah Silverman, really makes me laugh. Really sharp-eyed observational wit is great. But, at the same time, really creative comedy is a big interest of mine. You know, I started out doing standup as kind of a hobby, and I have to admit my biggest influence is the stand-up of Woody Allen because it was so creative and so different. It wasn't just looking at little aspects of his own life and talking about them. Every comedian is like a lowercase Jerry Seinfeld. They're all just talking about their own life with the benefit of Jerry's point of view. So, I don't know what makes me laugh from day to day, but I'm always on the lookout for real wit.

ALBRECHT: You are making me think of my class. In a class of twenty-five students, there are always one or two that just have wit. It is like they are just born with it, and people are gravitated to it.

MEHLMAN: I think if you are a kid and say something and the entire class laughs, it is pretty intoxicating.

ALBRECHT: Do you have a favorite episode of *Seinfeld*? Or, if you need to, let's go funniest and favorite?

MEHLMAN: Favorite would be "The Deal." Jerry and Elaine try to have sex and maintain their friendship. I think their negotiation of how they could do it—I think that scene was the best written scene in the history of sitcom. It was perfect in what *Seinfeld* characters were trying to do. They were always trying to create an ideal world, which is impossible to do. They never said the word *sex*. Jerry just points to the bedroom and says, "Why can't we just take what we have here, and just add that." And "The Contest" is probably the most purely funny episode ever. You know, I wrote the first freelanced episode they ever produced. It was in the first season, which was only thirteen episodes long. Once they accepted my script and put it on the schedule, they wanted me to come see the taping of all the other shows. If they got picked up, I would be on the show the next year and maybe have a better idea of what I am doing. So, I was actually in the audience for "The Deal." For "The Contest," I was the co-executive producer, or something, not that the titles meant anything.

ALBRECHT: Did the show and the humor change as its popularity grew?

MEHLMAN: You know, I left right before the last season. In fact, the last episode I wrote was "Yada, Yada." It is a real comedy of manners and small slice of life stuff that just blew up. I was happy to get out on something like that. The one time I got completely away from Jerry's apartment and coffee shop was the Hamptons episode with "Shrinkage."

ALBRECHT: That was your idea too?

MEHLMAN: Yeah.

ALBRECHT: I heard Elaine shoving people saying, "Get OUT!" was yours too? Is that true?

MEHLMAN: I think that there was one early script that I did that, and she went kind of up to Jerry and pushed him and said, "Get Out!" But I never really thought of that as one of my catch phrase inventions.

ALBRECHT: Double-dipping?

MEHLMAN: You know, if you come up with an idea like *double-dipping*, that's the hard part. The phrase "double-dipping" is the easy part. It doesn't take any great genius once you've come up with the idea to name it. I mean, it's a little harder with things like *sponge worthy*. That was a thing of the show, trying to come up with terms for things that really had no adjective or description of what they were.

ALBRECHT: Okay, a total switch of gears—favorite teacher. Do you have a favorite teacher?

MEHLMAN: I had a journalism professor in college who had been a writer for the LA times. His name was Dr. Lee Brown at the University of Maryland. He had covered the Los Angeles riots in the 60s, and he was really influential for me. It was a tough class because the main thing of the class was you had to write forty articles, basically three pieces per week for the student newspaper. I had already been on the student newspaper, so they gave me the best beat covering student government. I ended up writing, like, sixty articles that semester. It wasn't so much what he taught me. It was more about inspiration. He just inspired me to just turn out stories. The way things are now, people are always asking me about advice on a writing career, and that is a really hard question, but the one thing I always say is you just got to keep turning out stuff because eventually, maybe the really right person will read it. So, by putting out a lot, you are just increasing your chances of getting lucky, and getting lucky is everything.

ALBRECHT: That's true, being in the right spot at the right time is lucky.

MEHLMAN: You know, nobody wants to hear that, but there's a lot of luck involved. There is. I always hate those questions about "how do you break into sitcom writing" because they are going to ask how I did it. There is so much luck involved that they are going to be depressed by my answer. It's not like your dream is to be an investment banker, that you study really hard, go to a good business school, do well, and get your MBA, you're going to be hired by Goldman Sachs. It just doesn't work that way in creative fields. You just have to put out product and content and hope for the best.

ALBRECHT: So, taking away career aspirations, if you have one piece of advice for the world, what would it be?

MEHLMAN: I would say, try to be aware of what inspires you, because without being inspired, there is no hope. You have to find what inspires you and chase after it. If you are lucky enough to know what you want, then just start doing it. If you want to be a film maker, take out your film and make film. If you want to be a writer, sit down and write. It is not about putting out a resume and learning exactly what a teacher is telling you. It's more about keeping your brain open for business, doing what you want to do, and not being deterred because there are going to be potholes along the way. Don't be completely wedded to what you think you want to do next. Sometimes you can be pushed in another direction, and you find out that this is the way to go. Again, there is a lot of luck involved. And there is one other piece of advice: don't be scared to get in over your head. When I started with *Seinfeld*, I didn't know anything about dramatic structure. I didn't know anything about script writing, but, you know, you need to have a little blind confidence in yourself.

- **2** -

MY FRIEND ROSEMARY retired the same year a 150-year-old sugar maple tree had to be taken down in front of the most historical building in my town. Rosemary had been teaching biology at the high school for over thirty years, and her room looked like a science lab at the Smithsonian. It was full of an eclectic collection of beehives, plants, bones, skins, and a distinct smell that only organic matter can give off. If you are a teacher with a sensitive nose, never request a room in the biology wing of a high school. There are no rules for retirement other than a letter of intent. Most teachers leave behind almost all their collection of stuff in the closets, cabinets, and on the shelves. Thirty years of collecting nature's creations cannot simply be tossed into the dumpster, so most teachers leave their assemblage to the next poor soul to go through in hopes that something will be of value.

For years, my fourth-grade class had a bond with Rosemary's environmental club. In the fall, Rosemary would get over one hundred rainbow trout eggs. They were raised in a fifty-four degree cold water fish tank—another piece of the odor factory coming from her room. Rosemary decided to retire, and suddenly the phone rang during my language arts class. Some people understand to not call during class. Other people get something in their head and just call. Most calls start something like, "Are you teaching right now?" I try to remain polite, but inside I usually think, *no, I am picking my nose and drinking gallons of coffee. I decided to do nothing today and just let the kids play. What do you think I am doing?* Rosemary reminded me once again that she was retiring and started reminiscing about all the trips that my class took with her environmental club up to Lake Ontario to release the trout. Most teachers know me as the person that never says *no*, and that is how my classes and I started going on these trout releases to begin with. That day, in the middle of teaching about prepositions, Rosemary said, "I think that you should take the coldwater trout tank." Maybe she knew what she was doing. I was in a rush to get back to my prepositional phrases, and she was one heck of a saleswoman, so I said, "Sure, send it over at the end of the year." Without knowing it, I was in way over my head.

The average bathtub holds about twenty-five gallons of water. This fish tank holds 100 gallons. Plus, it had a noisy refrigeration system. When I arrived back to school in August, I felt like I was at Sea World. A fish tank of this size totally changes the configuration of a classroom. About a week after I put the fish eggs into the tank, we had a staff meeting. The conversation started with *I think a mouse died in the wall.* It turned out, there was no mouse—it was something that came with the tank—odor.

Peter Mehlman contradicted my entire fatherhood and teaching philosophy. I spent decades warning kids to not get in over their heads; Mehlman believes that no one should fear getting in too deep. When the fish tank began to make our hallway smell like forest rot, I thought my colleagues were going to toss me and my smells out the second story window. Until I spoke with Mehlman, I have always used the same line with my students and my own three children: *don't get in over your head.* Is Mehlman right? Is it better to sometimes get in over your head?

The day I discovered the fish tank in my room, Rosemary started screening her calls. There was no getting rid of the aquarium. The people from the Fish and Game Commission were coming with eggs, and I had a tank to prepare. Rosemary left me no directions and no advice, just a tank and a refrigeration system. I was in over my head. However, Mehlman offered one other insight. When he first arrived on the set of *Seinfeld*, he had never written a script in his life. Within months, he wrote some of the most iconic lines in the history of sitcoms. Mehlman scratched himself a note: *shut up and listen.* When Rosemary's fish tank showed up, I shut up and listened. I read, I called, and I listened. I also bought all the teachers in my school wing some Febreze.

In the previous chapter, I wrote about how my students write a letter to themselves that is returned to them their senior year. Many write about the fish release, and even teachers come to see the fish grow. The night custodian comes in each evening to give me a therapy session, while she sits in the comfy chair by the fish tank. When a kid has a meltdown, I take them to look at the fish. After talking with Peter Mehlman, I realized something: I need to tell kids to get in over their heads more often. Doing that pushes us out of our comfort zone and may just make each of us—and the people around us—a little crazy. Would I have ever just bought a hundred gallon fish tank with a refrigeration system? Absolutely not. It is way outside of my understanding and comfort. However, having it has created lifelong memories. So did Mehlman's shows. What is impossible at first becomes second nature as time goes on. Impossible is just a word for a challenge that nobody has ever taken on and achieved.

Luck plays a huge roll in many people's lives. Being in the right place at the right time happens often, and though we hope all the work we do to advance our careers and situations pays off, there is a lot left up to chance. How do we increase our odds in the game of life? Mehlman says that you need to *Keep your brain open for business.* The seeds of this statement most likely were germinated right in Dr. Lee Brown's class at the University of Maryland. If a semester is four months long, and Mehlman produced sixty articles that semester under Dr. Brown, then he was writing articles at an average of one every two days.

If I go to the gas station and buy one scratch off ticket, I may win, but my odds are low. What if I buy sixty tickets? Sooner or later, if I keep investing in lottery tickets, one is going to pay off, but there is no guarantee. Mehlman's advice is a lot like the lottery. The more you work, the more you put your brand out there, and the greater the odds are that you will get lucky. But there are no warranties on hard work. Luck and timing are real factors of success. A person like Mehlman could be the funniest creative genius in the world, but if he does not work daily to produce his best work, he will likely remain anonymous. The more you produce, the more likely you will be to find success, but laziness does not increase your chances. As chances increase, so do hope and purpose.

Many times per day, people have a choice to create or crumble. Both options come with a cost, but what is overlooked is the consequence of choices. Some people who are highly successful are crumbling, but money hides the fractures in their lives. They have developed a pattern of paying others for success. Creating an idea or an item takes time, education, and skill. The discomfort is paid up front, but it pays dividends later because the product is the work of the individual. Peter Mehlman gives us some advice about creating that a world full of tunnel visioned people can benefit from—*do a little bit each day*. He advocated for daily writing.

The more instantaneous the world becomes, the greater the challenges become for individuals to find a pace and a pattern to create. Creation should be a daily ritual that is done at a sustainable tempo. If it is not, eventually most people will abandon what they are doing. Every mountain climber starts their journey with a first step. Whether paying for others to create or procrastinating the start of fulfilling dreams, a first step has to be made. Exercise, eating habits, employment, education, and how free time is spent all tug at everyone's 'crumble: create ratio'. The ease of take out versus preparing a meal is a daily struggle for working adults. The ease of fast food, precooked meals, or dining out comes with greater financial discomfort and possibly changes in health. The crumble is always felt after the easier road is taken.

What we do with our free time is another story. As we get wrapped up in internet surfing, Netflix marathons, and compulsive eating, are we taking the time to truly listen to ourselves?

Or are we being told what to listen to? Are we searching in the correct places to find what inspires us, or has comfort and ease become an obstacle to seeking our passions? It is so easy to turn on a television. It is not easy to push ourselves to try new things or seek out inspiration. Hope takes work.

How much time do we listen to the rest of the world versus ourselves? We live in an instantaneous world. If you want to know something, pull out your cell phone and Google it. Whether we order fast food, get free overnight delivery, or use anticipatory software to write faster, we live like flashes of lightning. A faster pace makes things less meaningful. People are on to the next moment before the current one ends. Multitasking is the norm. Mehlman challenges us to be observers, not just of the world around us, but of the life within us. Instead of looking for inspiration on a computer, Mehlman creates original thought because he is guided by his inner voice. We all have one, but do we listen to it? Boredom occurs when we fail to identify what inspires us. Our society seems to have this idea that inspiration must be found in a career path. If a person is fortunate enough to have this intersection, they have scratched the winning lottery ticket. Winning the lottery is rare, so most people go to a job they can deal with but do not love—and that is okay! It puts food on the table and a roof over our heads.

Peter Mehlman spent a significant amount of time writing comedy. He also knew when it was time to move on to something different. With one season left, Mehlman decided to stop writing for *Seinfeld*. It is a good lesson. We must continue to reevaluate our lives if we are to continue the pursuit of our dreams. Each day we change a little, and over years a little change becomes significant. A simple parable I once heard went something like this: Some people visited a man who always gave good advice.

They came complaining about the same problems over and over, and they were never coming closer to answering their problems as they rehashed them. One day, the wise man decided to tell the group a joke, and they all roared with laughter. A few minutes later, he told them the same joke again. Only a few within the group giggled and one or two smiled. A few more minutes passed, and he told the same joke for a third time. No one laughed or smiled anymore. Many of the people looked confused, some appeared annoyed, while others were disinterested. The wise man smiled and said, "You can't laugh at the same joke over and over, so why are you always crying about the same problem?" It is easy to get stuck in a rut. A conscious and clear decision must be made to pursue our dreams, and the path that takes us there is full of obstacles and challenges. Bulldoze them with hard work! Create the path that leads to the discovery of hope and purpose.

- 3 -

I WAS PETRIFIED on August 25th, 1995. I had two things on my mind as I sat in our wood paneled station wagon in the parking lot of New Martinsville School. It was the first day of my teaching career in a public school. I briefly considered just pulling out of the parking lot and hiding somewhere. I was nervous and scared. I was also dead broke. I had been working as a lifeguard the whole summer. The pool manager kept a quarter from every hour each employee worked, holding us hostage until summer's end. If I held on until the end of the summer, I got my quarters. My wife and I each lost twenty to thirty pounds eating only Wonder Bread, cucumbers, and spaghetti for months.

As I sat there, I looked at my pants. They were olive green— not my choice. I had lost so much weight that summer that I had to buy new clothes. I guess olive green was fashionable in the 1970s, because twenty years later, the Salvation Army had a whole assortment of pants and shirts in that color.

Why was I scared? I had gone to college and had a master's degree under my belt. Was this not what I wanted all along? It was the first day of my career—I was supposed to be psyched. There is a point in all people's lives when we just want to bail out. We know the workload, pressures, and confusion that lay ahead. At that moment, I was most likely wearing a person's pants that were donated upon their death, a button down shirt that had ring around the collar, and a new lunch bag. I was on very unsteady ground. I had no friends in the building I was about to enter and never even imagined that I would be teaching in a middle school. I was not even certified for this job.

Your hope will be tested daily, and there are times that saunas will feel cold compared to the heat of a challenge. I already had sweat stains before 8:00 AM. Years later, I realize that opening that car door and getting myself into my windowless classroom was not comfortable, but it was the first step in my career. I was discovering my hope and purpose. I felt like I might as well have been walking on the moon. Hope is never easy, and sometimes it can feel downright mean in the moment. All you can do is put in the hard work to move forward. Had I pulled out of that parking lot, I would have driven away from hope, but I would have also avoided a major nightmare that happened during second period.

When I was hired, I was told that I was going to be teaching halftime middle school technology. I had no certification in this area, but in 1995, nobody did, especially in Appalachia. Thanks to some MIT professor named Tim Berners-Lee, the whole world was no longer concerned about learning Spanish. HTML was the new foreign language. To say I was building my airplane as it was hurtling down the runway was optimistic. I still really do not know why I was hired. My guess is there was no one else. I was young and eager to learn, surviving off the cheapest food known, and they needed a technology person. Problem solved for both of us—except my computer experience was nearly non-existent.

First period, I handed out floppy disks; there were no clouds or shared servers in 1995. We had RAM, but each student had their own issued floppy disk. Servers were small and did not contain a lot of storage space. First period seemed to go smoothly. *Okay*, I thought, *I have got this*.

The biggest error teachers can make is when over-confidence enters our minds, and that inner voice tells us *I solved it*. A quarter century of teaching has brought me to this conclusion—the moment you say *I solved it*, something bad is about to happen. I was a rookie on his first day. There was no way to see the next twenty minutes coming. Back in the 1990s, there was a term we called sagging. All the rappers' pants sagged to about halfway down their butt, so of course it was the cool thing to do. Due to an unwanted form of starvation over the summer, I had no butt. I was thin, but I guess I was cool because a seventh-grade girl said to me, "Sagg'n." Suddenly my Salvation Army one dollar pair of olive green pants were cool. I was sagging! Again, I thought, *I solved it. I am now the greatest teacher on the planet because I can relate to fashion. I sag!*

There is a scene in the movie *A Christmas Story*, that makes a lot of sense here. The family had just celebrated Christmas, everyone got what they wanted, and all was right in the world. Then, disaster struck. In the movie, the Bumpus hound dogs break into the house in the midst of all that is good and devour the Christmas turkey. In my case, it all started with those darn pants. In the parking lot they had seemed like an embarrassment, but by second period, I was feeling pretty good.

Shortly after I'd been labelled "sagg'n," the box of floppy disks got bumped onto the floor. Unlike elementary school kids who swarm like bees in the event of a spill, middle schoolers walk right over the mess. I was picking up disks when my newly beloved green pants split. They ripped *bad*. They were old, their time had come, and unfortunately, they had chosen to die during second period. The rip was where my missing butt should have been, approximately four inches long, and though middle school students were oblivious to the dropped supplies, they were highly observant to the sound of a ripped pair of pants. Seventeen students and me, all in a room, and my sagging pants were ripped in the wrong place.

There was a decision I had to make at this point, and it was more important than that moment in the parking lot—I could run, or I could laugh. I am not naturally funny around adults. I do better with little kids, but in this moment, I became the Einstein of creativity. I excused myself, took the newly ordered stapler, went into the bathroom, and "sewed" my pants with a Swingline. A stapler literally saved my ass that day. I learned two more valuable fashion tidbits that day—untucked shirts are cool, and so are rolled up sleeves. I did this to hide my unconventional tailor job, but I was told by a bunch of adolescents that I was the first teacher that *got it*. To them, an untucked shirt was cool. To me, it was a reminder: all those students knew I ripped my pants, and I was very embarrassed. My wife and I were living below the poverty line, and I was trying desperately to hide it. I wanted to be a teacher like everyone else, but the truth is, I was not. I was a twenty-three-year-old kid that knew nothing. I needed to look in the mirror.

Middle schoolers are ruthless. I returned to class wearing my freshly adapted seamstress job, and the students laughed. This is where hope in my career was born. That August 25th, sometime between 9:30 AM and 10:30 AM, I discovered hope. When I walked back into my classroom, I knew they knew. I could have run, cried, hid, or showed frustration. Instead, I laughed, and I still have no idea why. I threw out my plans and my perfect day and told the kids what I was hiding. I was twenty-three years old, I shopped for clothes at the Salvation Army because I had no money, and I just stapled my pants together. What did my students do? They laughed, but it was not at me. They laughed because I was real and funny. Peter Mehlman called this wit. Wit develops hope. Over fifty percent of the kids in that class came from homes that were in poverty. I admitted what I feared, and I knew what I had no control over. It was funny. I split my pants.

I am a lot older now. If my pants split, it would probably be because I have gained weight. I have learned that funny moments, laughter, and a little chaos is okay, both in a classroom and life in general. Last year I attended a workshop focused on anxiety in kids. Just the mere mention of the thought of kids with anxiety gives me shivers. They are only children after all—but it is frighteningly real. I am not an expert, but I learned that under stress, the body secretes hormones that can cause problems. Laughter reduces the level of stress hormones like cortisol and adrenaline. It also increases the level of health-enhancing hormones like endorphins and improves the number of antibody-producing cells. Science has proven the positive effects of laughter on the human body; twenty-six years of teaching experience has taught me the same thing.

I collect the best of all religious practices. Proverbs 17:22 in the Christian Bible reads, "A joyful heart is good medicine, but a crushed spirit dries up the bones." Are you happy in school or your workplace? Do you laugh there? If not, you do not necessarily have to leave. Rather, do something about it. The rediscovery of hope is not about abandoning what is broken. The challenge is to stay in the game. One way to guarantee that hope and purpose are not discovered is by fleeing the scene. There are times where the discovery of hope and purpose is analogous to a fireman entering an inferno. Laughter feeds the soul, creates purpose, and brings joy to our lives. It is by no means easy. One of the ways we can face our fears and demons is by laughing with them.

Giving up is far too easy. Discovering hope and purpose quickly is like trying to spring up a mountain. To be successful, a comfortable pace needs to be found. Effort, especially when a person is tired, scared, or lacks vision, is not easy. Life is simple during a winning streak. A life of hope and purpose takes sustained effort in a similar direction over a sustained period to even see a glimmer, and when the awkward moments happen, humor has its role. Do you laugh? If not, work on it. In doing so, you will be developing the hope that lives in your soul.

Chapter 7
Free is the Price of Hard Work

"We had talented players, but the whole came to exceed the parts, primarily because of their mutual devotion to a common cause."

-Tom Osborne

- 1 -

The easiest way to compare two coaches is by their statistics. A winning record exceeding eighty-three percent over the course of twenty-five years at any level in any sport is rare. As the head football coach of the University of Nebraska, Tom Osborne achieved that level of success, coupled with three national championships, numerous conference titles, and fifty-three All-Americans, including a Heisman Trophy winner. Multiple universities across the United States will pay millions of dollars for a coach who has attained this level of accomplishment.

In 1997, Osborne would win his final national title and retire from coaching football. He would teach at the college level until 2000. That year, he successfully ran for the United States Congressional seat of the 3rd District of Nebraska. Osborne won that office collecting eighty-three percent of the popular vote. Becoming a congressman takes a lot of time and money. Having left football, Osborne was sixty-three and headed to Washington. Though coaching and politics both require leadership, Osborne's change of career seems like a complete 180.

Once a person is established, why would they change? Does a significant intentional change later in life develop one's sense of hope and purpose? In this interview, Tom Osborne discusses his understanding of what it means to serve, what his greatest feelings of success are, and how this relates to the understanding of hope and purpose.

ALBRECHT: I appreciate you taking the time with me. You have done a lot of things in your life. You have been a football coach and a politician. With all this experience, how would you define yourself?

OSBORNE: Well, my main identity would be as a coach. As far as something I spent the most time at, I was a coach for thirty-six years, and that was the most meaningful thing I did. So, that has been the main emphasis of my life—working with young people.

ALBRECHT: What made coaching so meaningful for you?

OSBORNE: Well, I think you can make a difference in the lives of football players—in my case, young people. One time I got to talking with Tom Landry. Tom told me that in all the years of coaching in the NFL, he didn't feel he made a difference in the basic character of one of his players. By the time he got many of them, their character was pretty well-formed. I think probably in high school coaching you can make even more impact, but I felt when young guys came to us at seventeen or eighteen, that they were still kind of in the process of learning how to be an adult, and I thought of it as probably a time when I could make a difference in how they saw the world, world view, their value system, and what was important to them.

ALBRECHT: How would you define service?

OSBORNE: I think essentially, that in my experience that there is a temptation. I think we are all born with it—to be primarily self-serving, to take care of ourselves first. But I don't think that ends up being a very satisfactory way to live. I think that long term, long haul, it's somewhat like Mother Theresa said at one time, she said, "Unless a life lives for others, it's not worth living." That's kind of an extreme statement, but I think essentially that's kind of how we're built. The more we draw things to ourselves and try to advance ourselves, probably the less effective and maybe the less satisfied we are. I think to live a meaningful and purposeful life primarily is to help other people and make their lives better. That's essentially what we are here for.

ALBRECHT: Where do you think that should be taught?

OSBORNE: I think that it is caught more than it is taught by example, and certainly you can advance with principles in a school building. Probably, it's something that is mostly absorbed in the family. There are some people that never come to that way of thinking, so there is no sure way that will ever transpire.

ALBRECHT: You defined yourself as a coach. You have been a congressman. I am sure that in these roles you have come with a lot of experiences. Can you think of one example that you have witnessed as an act of service that would be a cornerstone of your belief?

OSBORNE: Well, I think that some of the best teams I had eventually arrived at a point where the welfare of the teammates, love for the team, exceeded personal ambition with a great majority of players. I don't think that you can totally remove that, but I think we live in a culture in which sometimes it is very much *me first*. The world of athletics can certainly be that way. We had a run in the mid-nineties where we won sixty games and lost three. I think the hallmark of those teams was that they had so much pride and devotion to the welfare of the team that they would sacrifice greatly—the amount of effort and training they put in. Many of the guys were on the scout team for three or four years. It meant a great deal to them to be part of the organization, and so that was one example where we had talented players, but the whole came to exceed the parts, primarily because of their mutual devotion to a common cause.

ALBRECHT: How do you define and understand the word hope?

OSBORNE: Hope is an attitude toward the future where you feel that things can get better, that you can make things better. Your life will transcend some of the difficulties you are facing. Hope is very powerful because when you lose hope, things tend to spiral downward pretty quickly. I remember one of my professors in college, graduate school, a guy named Don Clifton, he founded what is now Gallop. He did a study of prisoners of war—throughout all of our wars. He noticed in the Korean War that thirty-eight percent of the prisoners of war eventually died, which was the highest percentage of any prisoner of war population in the United States history of all our wars. It was a very negative environment where people informed on each other and eventually they lost hope. They weren't tortured. They weren't slaughtered or beaten, but eventually the negative environment led to a lack of hope. Hope is really important. Most leaders that are able to inspire people to see a better future, how things can get better, how they can make things better, are people who are most effective in the long run.

ALBRECHT: Do you see a connection between being a person of service and hope?

OSBORNE: I do. You know, my faith is very important to me, and essentially that is what Jesus was all about—being a man for others and serving other people. Eventually, those who followed him developed a strong sense of hope, partly in an afterlife, partly in terms of a better and more satisfying way to live. So, that has been a big part of my world view and how I see things.

ALBRECHT: You originally defined yourself as a coach. After you finished coaching, you went on to serve as a congressman. You could have stopped working in 1997, having won a national title. Instead, you chose to keep working so hard. Why?

OSBORNE: The representative from the third district [in Nebraska]—primarily a rural area representing eighty percent of the land mass of Nebraska had retired. That's where I grew up. That's where I have my roots, and I thought maybe I could help make things better with an area of the state that was not as affluent as Lincoln and Omaha, the eastern part of the state. I always felt that if you looked at the Founding Fathers—people who had started the country, they came from all walks of life. They went to Congress for three years, four years, or five years. Then they went back and resumed their normal life. It wasn't a career for them. I thought that maybe I could serve the people of that area, and so I did. I was there for three terms, and then I ran for governor and got beat. That was part of my life that I wouldn't say was the best part, but it was meaningful. I learned a lot. I was able to be of service, but I wouldn't choose politics as a long-term way of life.

ALBRECHT: I would guess it is definitely more fun on a football field than in an office.

OSBORNE: [with a chuckle] Yeah.

ALBRECHT: Do you have a favorite teacher?

OSBORNE: Hmmm… well, you learn from lots of people, not necessarily in a formal classroom setting. When I was in college there was a professor named Betty Bowen. She taught English literature. She was just a very kind and caring person. I remember her fondly. I had another professor named Darrell McFarren who was a history teacher. Those people didn't make much money. In those days they were very dedicated, very good and solid people. I went to a small school, Hastings College. I would say those were probably my two favorite professors. Again, I have learned a lot from a lot of people as time goes by. I actually was a teacher. I taught four years when I was doing graduate school at the university. A year or so after I got out of coaching, I was teaching. I did the same one year after I got out of politics. I have always enjoyed teaching, and it has been an important part of my life.

- 2 -

MANY PEOPLE SPEND incredible amounts of time coming up with reasons to not do things, but there are rare people out there that challenge and dare to bend the status quo. With the right mindset, people have done much of what was once considered impossible- flight, sailing around the world, a woman running a marathon, and an African American serving as the President of the United States. The impossible just means that there is more challenge than anyone has ever taken on. Stretching the boundaries of what can be done reminds me a lot of watching a child step to the edge of a diving board for the first time. There is hesitancy, needed encouragement, fear, and if the child jumps, a suspense of time. However, the second jump off the diving board is so much easier. People who dare to expand the horizon of our human vision are the tour guides for rediscovering hope and purpose.

Tom Osborne was sixty when he retired from coaching. He walked away from a job he loved where he was highly successful and respected. Following his last game, he earned an NCAA Division I championship trophy for the Nebraska Cornhuskers football team. It seems so utterly counterintuitive in today's world to leave when things are good. Is it really a good idea to walk away from a life at a high point? To many of us, this does not only seem like a bad decision—it seems impossible. This is where Osborne provides a roadmap that shows how the impossible is achievable.

Osborne proudly identifies himself as a coach to this day. His decision to continue teaching in college classrooms and then to serve as a congressman creates an understanding of how Coach Osborne spent thirty-six years of his life in sports in the first place. If the championships were his ultimate goal, surely he had the talent and vision to continue heading a premier football program well into the next millennium. He chose not to. The winning was about the team, not the individual. Osborne did not take the spotlight off himself. Rather, he always shared it with his players. In a world that is all about *me*, Osborne held on to the principle of *us*. He referred to a conversation he had with NFL Hall of Fame coach, Tom Landry. Landry struggled to guide some of his players who had established their routines. Osborne saw the potential in helping to guide young men to build a pattern of making healthy life decisions. He guessed that a high school coach may have an even greater impact because the athletes are still young and forming their self-identities. Hope and purpose are defined by the team, not the individual, but there needs to be a leader to teach this.

Was Osborne a football coach or a life coach? He was both. Osborne chose to use football as a teaching medium for serving his players. Could doctors, custodians, business owners, teachers, or any professional have the same mindset? Absolutely. When we go to work, is the job about *what you do* or *how you do it*? Service mindedness is transferrable; it is not glued to one profession. It is a simple act for the owner of a company to walk through the factory each day and talk to his or her employees. It takes very little for a teacher to pick up the phone and check in on a family when that teacher's gut instinct tells him that a mom or a dad is wondering how their child is doing at school. No harm is done by a doctor following up with a patient because she is concerned. Osborne quoted Mother Theresa. I will, too. Mother Theresa also said, "It is not great things that make one great. It is little things done with great love." The Founding Fathers of the United States were farmers, lawyers, doctors, businessmen, writers, and merchants. The apostles of Jesus were tax collectors and fishermen; Simon was a zealot, and Judas could be defined as a thief. A person's life circumstance does not have to define them. Leaders and those that guide others can come from all walks of life. Definition comes from the values that are upheld.

When I first began preparing for my conversation with Tom Osborne, I was looking for a person who made a full 180-degree turn in life. I believed that redefinition created cracks in which hope and purpose could grow. Osborne went from being a highly successful coach at the University of Nebraska to a three-term United States Congressman. I wrongly inferred Osborne entered politics to serve the interests of his congressional district in Nebraska. He did not enter politics to begin a life of service. He entered politics because all along he had been a man of service as a football coach. What I did not consider was that his value system of hope was not defined by a desire to suddenly serve. His success in coaching proved that hope was always there.

How old is too old to change? Osborne admitted that as athletes grew older, they became harder to guide in their life-decisions. Change seems easier when a person is young, though at age sixty, Osborne seemed alright with a change. It certainly was not easy, but his focus on the way he lived his life—not on his accomplishments—created a world where he was not redefined by his career because his general principles stayed the same. He served students as a teacher, and he served the people of Nebraska's 3rd Congressional District as a congressman. What looks like a 180-degree life change was actually quite linear because Osborne's devotion to service did not vary.

Television captures the media coverage of products—championships and election results. What is not seen or heard are the conversations with players in the coach's office, the actions during practice, comments written on students' assignments, or the personal moments when a congressman visits with farmers in rural Nebraska. No age is too old to make what appears to be major change on the outside if the fundamentals of a person remain consistent on the inside. Only death makes you too old for a change. Occupational routines may be hard to break, but if the mission is consistent, what appears to be a major difference may simply be a different manner of service. The name *Coach* Osborne is an endearing and special name for him. He does not wear that badge of distinction the same way he wears *Congressman*. The joy of a job is dependent on the individual. When asked who his favorite teacher is, he said that he has learned a lot from many people. This path of lifelong learning extends into his life post-coaching. Another founding principal of Osborne is to live life as a learner.

A successful career, lifestyle, or location change does not define the individual making the change if the inherent values remain consistent. Change causes new growth and learning. New lenses are formed to look at the world and serve other people. We often see such major changes as a sign that something bad happened to cause the shift, but it does not have to be that way. A person can be happy and change careers. A coach can retire after winning national championships in three of his last four seasons. However, what cannot change are the guiding principles that make up the soul of a person. Institutionalizing the fundamentals of what guides a person, rather than the achievements he or she has accomplished, drives the rediscovery and maintenance of hope and purpose.

- 3 -

A HISTORICAL GLANCE at the year 1863 could potentially make the argument that not only is January 1st the beginning of a new year but also a day to celebrate freedom from the shackles of money. Few words ever get more attention than the word *free*. We have a kitchen counter that has never been used for food. It is loaded with piles of stuff. Most houses have a spot on a desk, shelf, closet, or counter which is a catch-all. It is the place that mail goes that cannot be filed or thrown out. Broken things that need to be glued, spare change, and random candies get buried there. Intermingled with all these miscellaneous items are items that were free. When I walk by a stand that reads free pens, free bracelets, or even free thumb drives, it all somehow makes it to that counter. None of it is needed, but the allure of *free* causes each bit of clutter to make its way to our household's pocket, and on the counter it lives.

Free trinkets are one thing, but free land would be hard to pass up. Daniel Freeman was born in Preble County, Ohio on April 26th, 1826 and was raised in the Genesee Country of New York. The stretch of land from Syracuse to Buffalo along the shores of the Lake Ontario watershed holds a rich bounty of soil. The dirt of Ohio and upstate New York had lured pioneers to begin the westward movement out of the rocky grounds of New England. Land tracts were buried under the dense growth of a virgin forest of poplars, elms, and oak trees. Trees were girdled, causing leaves to drop and bathe the valuable and rich soil in sunlight. Stumps were left in fields because there was no time to remove them, and farms were started in a Lorax-like setting.

In the spring of 1816, Mount Vesuvius erupted halfway around the world. The trade winds cause an almost unnoticeable fine coating of ash to remain in the air and encircle the earth, causing the summer temperatures in Genesee Country to never surpass seventy degrees. Four frosts had killed off all crops, and with the strong belief in omens and the work of the devil, many farmers died or moved on to Ohio. Like many early pioneers, rumors spread of greater opportunities in other places, so a semi-nomadic lifestyle was common. The Freemans were no exception. Because of the frequent movement, I would infer that Daniel Freeman was not bound by financial ties, but rather led a life of hope with the dream of prosperity. The Louisiana Purchase was only decades old; it was time to capitalize on that investment.

A soldier and volunteer in the 17th Illinois Volunteer Infantry Regiment during the Civil War, Freeman was well-educated, having graduated from a medical institute in Cincinnati, Ohio. This active regiment was part of the battles of Fredericktown, Shiloh, Thompson Station, Port Gibson, Raymond, Champion's Hill, the Little Black Hawk River, and the Siege of Vicksburg. Freeman had witnessed many defining moments in American history, including a national reexamination of core values. The Civil War was highly focused on core values, which varied greatly between North and South. People needed to ground themselves in the principles they were willing to die for. If there ever was a circumstance for developing hope, Freeman was right in the thick of it.

Timing is a variable that is not within our control. In chapter five, I interviewed Ken Deardorff. He was the final beneficiary of the Homestead Act. He would be close to the four-millionth homesteader to file a claim on a piece of free land. He was not trying to get into the history books as the last homesteader, but his timing made him such. Daniel Freeman would be the first. He filed a claim on a 160-acre stretch only ten minutes after midnight on January 1ˢᵗ, 1863. Homesteading is backbreaking work, and its success hinges on the effort of the homesteader and some luck with weather, injuries, and sickness.

On May 20ᵗʰ, 1862, President Abraham Lincoln unleashed a freedom and hope that America had never seen before and arguably will never see again. The act was simplistic. Starting January 1ˢᵗ, 1863, the Homestead Act—which was heavily supported by Lincoln's Republican constituency to the north—made it possible for 270 million acres of American public land to be claimed by any person willing to farm and live on the land for five years. The homesteader would be responsible for working on land improvements, the construction of a residency, and farming on the land itself. After five years, the full ownership of the land was transferred to the homesteader for a small fourteen dollar filing fee.

The legislation was gender neutral. New hope was on the horizon for men and women, but quick money was not to be made. Free land was a catalyst for the rediscovery of hope and purpose. Free giveaways crush hope. This land came without financial burden, but ownership did have a price—grit. Cultivating new land is backbreaking, and ownership meant commitment. Hope is not developed by taking the easy road. Lincoln's presidency would see the law passed, but southern Democrats such as James Buchanan had vetoed this legislation, adamantly insisting that this land be open to much more qualified people—particularly southern slave owners. There was a lot at stake. Nearly ten percent of America's landmass would be claimed during the 123 years of the Homestead Act.

Daniel Freeman's letters home indicated that he first identified his tract of land in June of 1862. Freeman had to file for military leave because claims needed to be made in person. To his surprise, leave was granted quickly, but there was a stipulation: he was to report back for active duty in St. Louis, Missouri no later than January 2ⁿᵈ, 1863.

Unfortunately, young Freeman did not consider that January 1ˢᵗ was a national holiday. He arrived by horse at the land office in Brownville, Nebraska to a wild New Year's party spread throughout the town. He wanted to be one of the first to have a crack at the prime land; the area he had selected offered fertile soil, a creek, healthy trees, and a developed road that led straight to the local railroad. As he stumbled through the crowd, Freeman came upon a group of sober men who offered him guidance. Office assistant Jim Bedford was the one to see, and in a stroke of luck, the man in question ordered Freeman to follow him to his office.

Freeman explained his Army orders and deadline. Bedford examined Freeman's paperwork and explained that January 1ˢᵗ was a holiday; the office would not be open until January 2ⁿᵈ. For Freeman, that would be too late; he was certain that if he did not secure the land that night, it would be taken from him. As he argued his case, the ruckus outside grew—January 1ˢᵗ, 1863 had arrived. Bradford gave in and signed the papers, giving a 160-acre parcel of land, hope, and purpose to Daniel Freeman with the simple stroke of his pen and a fourteen-dollar filing fee. That night, one of the most explosive expanses in human history began in a primitive dugout not far from Beatrice, Nebraska.

The land was almost free, but hope did not come free with it. Hope was discovered in every drop of sweat, every injury, and every blister on the farmers' hands. Like Tom Osborne's commitment to his principles of service across three different occupations, any homesteader would be successful only if they held true to the principles of tenacity, resilience, and willingness to take on hardship for the benefit of a future family. The land required challenge, commitment, and vision—which are, incidentally, essential ingredients of the rediscovery of hope and purpose. What would life have been like for those early homesteaders? This is how Beverly Kaplan, the great-granddaughter of Daniel and Agnes Freeman, described the early days:

> Cash was scarce. Until a crop could be grown, it would become scarcer. The sod had to be broken and the seeds dropped. Spring came early in 1865. The sod plow sliced through the roots of heavy grasses and chunks of black soil curled around the moulboard and dropped over burring the grass. The insects housed among the buried roots from their hiding and faced a bright April sun. In boots curled at the toes from many soakings and worn to the raw leather, Dan tramped behind in the narrow furrow. Spring bugs flitted past the mare's ears. The plow lay sliced through the slender damp roots. The meadowlarks strutted across the fresh plowed earth and filed upon the scurrying insects and the occasional white grubs.

> Every round he'd stop and pull the plow out of the ground and file the lay sharpener. It was brutal work for both horse and man. A half day's work gnawing through the tangle of grass roots would blunt the lay and make it necessary to pound it flat again. A couple of days plowing, and the share would have to be taken to town again for Jake Shaw to draw out in his sooty blacksmith shop.

Why not just get a job working for someone? Why start from scratch doing backbreaking and slow-paced work? Was all this done just to get a 160-acre farm? In the end, to see a working farm scratched out of raw earth by the work of beast and man grew more than crops. The value of incredibly hard work sewed seeds of hope and developed purpose in life.

Not everyone is a farmer. Freeman was also a sheriff, county coroner, and physician. If the internal ambitions of a person are founded in a system of consistent values, a diversity of occupations may not be as big of a deal as it initially seems. What is something that you are so passionate about that you would put your life's work into it, both mentally and physically? Fundamental principles should not vary, whether a person is an artist or an astronaut. It is up to the individual to define what morals they value and then stick to them for a lifetime. The path to hope and purpose is paved with each person's underlying principles and thoughts.

Chapter 8
Hope is Self-Serving When Serving Others

"Service to others seems the only intelligent choice for the use of wealth. The other choices, especially personal consumption, seem either useless or harmful."

-Manoj Bhargava

- **1** -

Manoj Bhargava is a billionaire businessman that breaks the norms of the ultra-wealthy. Whereas many foundations bear the name of their founders, Bhargava prefers to provide service to the world in a more discrete, conventional and practical way. His focus is on an understanding of basic human need, guided by his belief that serving others is as important to the soul of a person as breathing is to survival. Though he has his mind on many different ventures, projects, and innovations, his most recognizable product is found at the checkout lines in most major retailers and convenience stores. 5-Hour Energy drink—produced by his company, Living Essentials LLC—was launched in 2004. Within eight years, 5-Hour Energy drink's sales topped one billion dollars.

Bhargava is only one of a very charitable and elite group of the world's most wealthy people who have taken The Giving Pledge. The pledge is a publicly displayed moral commitment to give from a massive pool of acquired financial wealth with no legal contract. Though there is no formal agreement, the goal is to inspire the wealthy people of the world to give at least half of their net worth away through philanthropy, either during their lifetime or upon their death. The Giving Pledge's website displays letters written by participants explaining their logic behind their convic-

tion to give away what they worked for many years to earn and maintain. At the beginning of 2020, 209 individuals or couples had registered from twenty-three different countries, with ages ranging from people in their 30s to their 90s. Bhargava's message on the Giving Pledge website states:

"My choice was to ruin my son's life by giving him money or giving 90+% to charity. Not much of a choice. Service to others seems the only intelligent choice for the use of wealth. The other choices, especially personal consumption, seem either useless or harmful. The projects our foundation works on are defined only as alleviating human suffering. We have adopted over 400 charities from schools and hospitals to women's career education in rural India. We are also working on desalinating water cheaply, reducing fossil fuel emissions by 50%, cleaning mercury and sulfur dioxide from coal and a revolutionary medical technology that will improve overall health for the poor and the not so poor. For us, all this falls under reducing human suffering. We may not be able to affect human suffering on a grand scale, but it will be fun trying."

Is service mindedness connected to a person's rediscovery of hope and purpose? Does wealth come with obligation? If people are not wealthy, can they contribute? Bhargava's wealth is in the billions, yet he maintains a hands-on lifestyle. This was evident when a simple email to his administrative assistant led to my phone ringing in the middle of the day. It was not a secretary on the line; it was Manoj Bhargava himself.

ALBRECHT: Thank you for taking the time to call me. Here is why I have reached out to you. I am fascinated with you and what you are doing.

BHARGAVA: [laughing] I did that little documentary thing to see if people would help in what we are doing. It turns out that many people were interested in talking about it but not doing anything, so I took a step back and said, "I'm going to do it by myself." So, at this point I am outside of looking for publicity. I just assume to toil in obscurity if I could. If we get some great ideas, it's good. If not, that's okay. So, what would you like to know?

ALBRECHT: As a teacher, I like to ask anybody I meet, who is your favorite teacher?

Bhargava: Oh God, I was a monk for twelve years, so it wouldn't be a fair question because I was taught a whole different area where—it is more taught about fundamentals than it is about if you can acquire facts, so how to think was the bigger issue. It is a different discipline entirely. I would say if I would have to answer that question in one sentence, it would be the same for the best teachers.

ALBRECHT: Service is very important to you. Is that correct?

BHARGAVA: Well, I kind of look at it differently. I look at it as if you have something, then it is your duty to help others. It is not really *oh, you're doing a good thing*. It's sort of, no... does a mom do good things by taking care of her child? No. It's her duty. It's her job. She should do it. If she doesn't do it, then, that's a question. So, I don't look at service as [pause]... It should be part of you as a human being, not like you are doing a great thing to serve others. It needs to be taught at a level deeper than *to do good*. No, it should be built in. It should be taught to a level that if you are fortunate, then that's your job. It's your duty. It's not an extra thing, so I don't consider what I am doing better than anyone else because, what else would I do? I can do dumb stuff, or I can do this. There does not seem like a lot of choices here. I have nothing else to do.

ALBRECHT: I believe we share a similar passion. I have always felt funny about having clubs in school where there is a minimum requirement or a set total amount of hours of service. To me, service should be a lifestyle, and the person next to you is the most important person in the moment.

BHARGAVA: There are so many other issues that come from that. The way to be miserable is to think about yourself. The way not to be miserable is to think about others. [laughing] It is really that simple. These days it has to be all about me. That is the new fashion. Those are the people that are the most miserable. People who sacrifice for others are strongest. In a mental state, they are the strongest because they don't worry about themselves. They worry about other people. That is the path to strength. It sort of all fits together, so in a way, it becomes selfish. If you do the right thing, all good things happen. If you do the right thing, then the consequence of that is good, and if you don't do your job, then the consequences are not so good.

ALBRECHT: I believe what you are talking about is in line with what I am defining as the rediscovery of hope and purpose. What you are talking about is not just a mindset. It requires a lot of effort and work. It is a day-to-day grind, a lifestyle, and service is not just a one-shot deal.

BHARGAVA: That's right. I am kind of against the word, hope, but everything else, I agree with you. Hope, to me, is mostly greed. It is wishing for something more than you have. Instead, you should be satisfied with what you have, and work for others to do more for them. Hope always says *I need more*, so I don't really ascribe to that as much because no matter how poor or rich you are, you are always going to hope, which means you want more. The definition of that becomes a little "iffy" to me. What you hope, what you believe, what you say—to me, all of these are irrelevant. The only thing that matters is what you do.

ALBRECHT: I think that the interpretation of hope, the definition of hope and the semantics of what I am saying is more about *what is your purpose in the world?* What I have found is that people have defined hope in alignment of scratching a lottery ticket, people hope about getting a promotion at work, and that is truly not what hope is. Hope does not happen in a moment, but it is defined through serving others and identifying your personal purpose consistently over a lifetime. What you are saying is very confirming.

BHARGAVA: Okay, yup.

ALBRECHT: Would you tell about some of the work you are doing?

BHARGAVA: In my view, the biggest problem coming up, and it is already in a huge number of countries, is going to be water for both health and survival. So, we've created—we are just about to launch it here—we have created a box that is a little bit bigger than the size of a washing machine that will clean whatever kind of water to make it better than current bottled water. It will work in any village. It can be plugged even in on a 110 [referring to volts]. It requires less power than a hairdryer, and it can do ten gallons per minute, so we can clean—the biggest amount of water out there that is unusable is called brackish water. It's difficult to even acknowledge because it is worthless. It's useless. Now, it's in the middle of the country. It's slightly salty water. It's everywhere.

I had this really funny conversation with this guy, the richest guy in Indonesia, and I asked *do you have brackish water here?* He looked at me like *are you an idiot? That's all we have.* So, with a population of about 300,000,000 people, their water has pretty much run out, and they have brackish water, which they can't use. So, the biggest issue in certainly half of the world is water. In the United States, it is not so much. We have plenty of water here, but I found out that no water is clean. The incidences of things such as cancer is really based on water. If you go to the EPA website, you will see two columns. One column says what is good for you, and the other describes what can be allowed. They are really different from each other. And, on the ingredients of what is allowed, there is a label that says that *this causes this cancer, and this causes that cancer. This causes this long-term disease.*

We have created something that will fix all of that. We are sort of quietly—it is sort of a twenty-year project. To get it across the world is going to take twenty years. At this point, with these politicians, nobody is going to help, so the great challenge for me is that if nobody's helping... nope, nope, nope. It is a great challenge. It is a great opportunity. I say, "Okay, no problem. I'm going to do it myself. I just have to find a way to do it." I could make excuses, right, so you either do something or you make excuses, right? That's why we created this thing. For what it does, it is relatively inexpensive, and it lasts twenty years, so you have water that is going to be good everywhere. In places like southeast Asia, certainly, China, eighty percent of the water is bad, Indonesia, India, Africa, Sri Lanka, Bangladesh, there is just arsenic. Sixty to seventy percent of the population is sick because they are drinking arsenic. You can't stop drinking water, so all of that will be fixed. We're taking that approach, saying, *Okay, let's just do this one project. That's the biggest.*

We have a bunch of other things that we have done. Another big project that we have is we found out about the farmers worldwide. Poverty is within eighty percent of the farmers, so when I look at their problem, I said, "Okay, okay, what is this problem?" So, I found out that they basically make two percent on what they generate. The rest is eaten up by diesel, water, fertilizer, and something else. We found out that thirty percent of their money is going to fertilizer. We created this thing—we created a way that they could make their own fertilizer for free, and it improves the food. The raw materials are agricultural waste, which is dry waste, some green waste, which is leaves, water, a few other things, and some cow dung. It will make better fertilizer. The water requirements drop by forty percent because this fertilizer allows the water to be absorbed, whereas chemical fertilizer doesn't absorb water, so the sun takes it out. A big problem is water, and this stuff—it is free, so their wages go from two percent to a minimum of twenty-two percent. All of the sudden, they are out of trouble. So, we are working with 50,000 farms now. In the next ten years maybe, it will be a million farms. We are tackling stuff that is very fundamental. None of this is popular amongst the rich, because often, the rich don't really care about all this stuff. It is sort of like the news. One person dies that is rich, it is all over the newspaper for days, but a thousand people in Africa die, and nobody cares. It is not relevant. That's human nature, and I am not necessarily saying that is a bad thing. It is just the way that we humans are, but somebody has to get up and say *they're going to fix it,* but who is *they*? Somebody's got to say, *I am going to get up there and do it.* [laughing]

ALBRECHT: What you are saying sounds a lot like a classroom. We do not talk a long period of time about problems. We spend our time solving things.

BHARGAVA: The only difference is my scale is about a billion people. We do all kinds of crazy things. Our foundation—I feed a million kids a day. For many of them, it is the only meal they will get, but they have to come to school to get it. Education can be a byproduct of getting fed.

ALBRECHT: That is a huge concern we have as our schools have been out for an extended time with remote learning. The school is a safe place for many of these children, and they get fed a breakfast and a lunch. In our school, it is fifty percent. It is about life and death at this point.

BHARGAVA: I know that one. I know that one well. It is even worse in poorer places.

ALBRECHT: Okay, so you are able to support these programs because you have a lot of money. What would you say to a person like me that does not have as much? You said that support is an important thing. What would you say about how would somebody like me serve?

BHARGAVA: Everybody has some, whatever compacity of what you have or are given. Right? But, how much you get done—either you make excuses and say *I can't do it because I have so little* or you get out there and say *Okay, I have so little, no problem, I'll do as much as I can*, and that's all it is. I look at anybody's character, it is not about how much they have. If somebody gives ten dollars, it has value to them. I may give a million dollars and that comes easier to me than this guy's ten dollars. Again, we are talking about money, which I don't like to because I do not think it is all about money. There are guys that certainly have a hundred times the money that I have, but they're not getting much done. For example, I talk to Bill Gates and these other guys, and certainly, I am a poor guy compared to them. Then, I look at it and say, *No, no, it's whatever you've got, you have to think about it, use your brains, and say, what can I do?* It is too lazy to say, *Well, you know, I don't have that much, so I won't do anything.* Some of the laziest rich people are more involved in what the latest fashion is. In one case, I know of a person who tried to bring farmers toilets. The farmer said, *What? What I am I going to use that for? Just because things smell?* Some people just don't understand. We need to ask, *What do you need? You are the customer. What* *do you need?* Most people are kind of condescending. They look down at this guy and say, *I'll tell you what you need. I've got this study from Harvard.* That is idiotic.

It even took me a while. I am smart enough to figure out what a farmer or a poorer person needs, in one sentence? And almost no one at the nonprofits have figured that out. It really comes down to one thought—to make a living. The rest of it is all secondary—to get educated, to get this, to get medicine. Even medicine is secondary to making a living. If you don't make a living, it is the one before all of the zeros. Even in education, the first job is to make a living. If people say, *I didn't go to school to be a farmer.* I respond to those people and say, *So, you went to college. Do you know how to farm? No. He lives on a farm. He is educated at farming.* A person's first job is to get whatever education to feed himself and his family. After that, he can do everything else.

What we are dealing with are very fundamental things. What we are trying to create is so fundamental. One other thing we have, which we kind of put it on the backburner right now. We kind of created a box the size of a lunchbox what would give you electricity for twelve years with no bill. Once you have it, you will not have an electric bill. Now, you are not going to be running TVs off of it, but you can read, you can use a computer, or a cellphone or an iPad type thing for education. The thing that I looked at was, this is education. What is the first part of education? We gave this thing to a village; I remember because I went there twice. The first time that I went to the school, it was a tin roof with no walls a blackboard and some chalk. So, we gave them this box. The next time I came, they were on the internet! They went from chalk and board, skipped books, and went to the internet! What the fundamental of education became in this case was electricity. It was free. Books would cost money. They are not going to get books at this point. The only free thing was the internet. The fundamentals of all these challenges are different, so we're always looking at the fundamentals. There are some people doing the things that bring them glory. We are doing the things that bring us no glory, which suits us perfectly because I would just assume—I just want to be quiet.

ALBRECHT: What you are saying about necessities and root causes seem to be a very consistent message with those that are bringing hope to the world, and those root causes are often overlooked, but are very simple. Correct?

BHARGAVA: Almost always. If it is not simple, it is going to have unintended consequences.

ALBRECHT: So, one last question. If you had to give one piece of advice to the world, what would it be?

BHARGAVA: I don't have anything on that. Look, I try to do the best I can, and that's it. The rest, I don't teach, I don't do anything. You know, like teaching, you just walk the walk. First, just do stuff. Everybody else will follow that, and if they don't follow, that is fine too. You know, you just have to do those things that are worth doing. I don't pretend to be smart enough to advise the world. I just do my work.

ALBRECHT: Well, I have really enjoyed our conversation. I wish you continued luck in your mission.

BHARGAVA: I have too. Before you go, you know we did this documentary thing. I must tell you this story. We had to go to Singapore, and I am walking on this mall because everything is underground over there. There are two ladies, a mother with probably a fourteen-year-old. And, this girl approaches me and asks, "Are you Manoj Bhargava?" And, I thought, "What the hell?" At first, I thought *I am in a foreign country. I don't know anybody.* Then I found out that apparently, they taught that documentary in every school in Singapore.

ALBRECHT: So, you are inspiring people.

BHARGAVA: They actually came up with a curriculum for it. [laughing] I was so excited. The documentary was not intended for that, but in Singapore it was in their school.

- 2 -

BUZZY WAS THE janitor who swept the halls of my middle school. He was old when I first saw him—hunched over, expressionless, and always with a wad of tobacco between his cheek and gum. He had greasy hair pushed back and a belly. One day Buzzy saw me get spit on while walking the long, unsupervised hallway to wood and metal shop by "Brian the spitter." I took alternative routes to avoid Brian, but I was outright mortified of ever going near Buzzy. To me, Buzzy was a lunatic. He was an old-school custodian, through and through, and to me he seemed like a character straight out of a Stephen King book.

I never heard Buzzy speak until he cornered me. I doubt custodians of Buzzy's era ever received training on how to talk with adolescents. Without any preamble, he simply asked, "Do you fish?" At the time I remember being really confused. I thought I was going to get torn apart for not fighting back. What did fishing have to do with anything?

For over two years after that conversation, I spent nearly every Saturday, March through November, sitting on a five-gallon bucket catching carp, catfish, and an occasional bass out of the Erie Canal below the Parker Street bridge. I rode my Schwinn to the bridge, and Buzzy replaced his wad of tobacco with cigars. Buzzy was the polar opposite of wealthy, but he understood what he did have—time and companionship. Bhargava was very quick to identify that ten dollars to one person may be as much of a sacrifice as a million dollars is to him. Therefore, a simple mindset of sacrificing for others within one's means is the most important.

Eventually, Saturday morning baseball practices replaced two years of fishing, and I no longer saw Buzzy. I moved on to the high school. Between his cigars and hacking cough, my guess is that he is no longer on this Earth. Buzzy's wealth was his time without unnecessary conversation. In society's eyes, sadly, money seems much more valuable than anything Buzzy had to offer. Buzzy was unselfish with his time, and therefore, in the end, just as important as Manoj Bhargava. I am pretty sure Bhargava would agree. He understands that it is impossible to know what someone needs unless you ask them, visit them, and spend time with them. As he pointed out, if a solution is not simple, there often are unintended consequences.

In Bhargava's words, "People who sacrifice for others are the strongest." Bhargava has the privilege of money. He earned every bit of it with his many products, including 5-Hour Energy. It was an instant success. The moral question that he addresses without it ever being explicit is—*what is the obligation of any person if they have more than another person?* The response to this question should never be limited to money. The discussion within this interview revolved heavily around projects and philanthropy; the money was a means, not the solution. Money is tangible, and all people in the world know the pains and pleasures of its driving force.

Bhargava's story is, by default, sensationalized in most people's minds because he is giving away money, and lots of it! The population of the ultra-wealthy on Earth is only the tiniest fraction of people. Is charity only a duty of the rich? Not at all. All classes of people have an obligation to serve. There seems to be a stigma that time and money are the major players in the game of service. Most people are trying to make more money. They must write their lives down on calendar planners or plug their schedules into phones because people have become such complex creatures. We do not remember where to go and at what time. Living life for others needs to come before anything else. Ultimately, what we give should not be dictated by what we have, but rather by what others need. Hope and purpose are discovered when a person fulfills a need in another person. To understand the need, people need to observe.

Money is a large obstacle in the modern world. The path away from the discovery of hope and purpose is littered with dollar bills. The amount of money a person makes leads to career changes, irrational purchases, and ultimately misery. There are vast consequences, both positive and negative, associated with money, depending on how you choose to use it. As Bhargava stated, "The way to be miserable is to think about yourself. The way not to be miserable is to think about others." Why are so many people in this world miserable with their job? Millions go to work each day to do something they do not want to do, shackled by money and status. It is no coincidence that Bhargava coupled employment, good fortune, and duty together. If any of these pursuits are self-serving, he warns that they will make people miserable.

Bhargava understands that it is the duty of those who have more to share. This mindset is not a choice. A visionary can see beyond obstacles and deficiencies to find the simplest path to fill needs. To live a life of service does not mean throwing time and money at something that may not need either. Service mindedness is about asking questions, getting to root causes, celebrating history, observing, and creating simple solutions.

What is popular is not always right, and what is right is not always popular. Early in our discussion, Bhargava pointed out that many people like to talk about serving others, but when the time comes for action, few are willing to do what it takes. Does this matter? Not to him. Judgement of others puts a ball and chain on hope. If a person has belief in a mission, then other people's participation (or lack thereof) is irrelevant. There is always the option to take on challenges by ourselves. If an individual truly believes in their life's mission, and nobody is willing to walk with them, they still should keep going! The life's work of a person is not about publicity or popularity.

A phenomenon of habitual interruption and lack of attention has come with the growth of social media. It has become socially acceptable to take selfies and post the pictures online. Internet companies know this, and the practice of tagging others in photos has become a billion dollar per year business. People give away their trends to major companies who use the data to enter retail markets. The advertisement that is subtly embedded in what we read online gradually shifts our behaviors, purchasing habits and the way we spend our free time. Vanity promotes further vanity. Bhargava warns us that misery is promoted when people think about themselves, and the way to not be miserable is to think about others. He called that task simple. However, he has been classically trained as a monk educated in self-discipline.

In 1995, I began teaching technology to middle schoolers in West Virginia. That same year, the internet was being installed in classrooms nationwide. At the time, the biggest items in people's pockets were their wallets. In twenty-five years, those pockets have cellphones with wallets loaded on an application, which presents items to buy based on our behavior. Instant gratification is satisfied when kneejerk purchases are made. Technology has made it easier to gravitate toward the black hole of self-service.

Bhargava is quite serious about the power of money. In a short time, he confirmed that his wealth feeds millions per day. In the same breath, he discussed the pledge he has taken to give most of it away. He understands the destructive force it may cause to his family if they develop the addiction of allowing money to blind them from serving others. Like social media, money, if used improperly gets in the way of serving others. The accumulation of wealth is a practice that dates to a time before money was coined. The desire and pursuit of wealth is deep-rooted. Bhargava traveled that path of life. What makes him unique is his ability to responsibly let go of it before it corrupts him, his family, or the people around him.

On his twenty-five acre manufacturing facility, Bhargava has dedicated one of his ten buildings for work on his innovations that support his duty to the world. By accepting that other individuals do not share his vision, and by not worrying about whether others will join his charity, he realizes others do not have to define his hope and purpose.

No person on this planet is a clone of one another. Each living person is no more important than the next. A billionaire and a pauper are both born, and both will die. Therefore, only possessions cause inequity. Do a person's circumstances have to define them? Near the end of our interview, I asked Bhargava if he had one bit of advice for the world. Bhargava's response is unique. So many want to tell others how to live their lives. At a net value of over four billion dollars, it seems implausible that Bhargava has escaped this trap. Instead of telling others how to live their lives, he simply says, "You know, you just have to do those things that are worth doing. I don't pretend to be smart enough to advise the world, I just do my work."

- **3** -

HENRIETTA NESBITT GREW up in Hyde Park, New York and was a friend of Eleanor Roosevelt. A young Henrietta grew up by modest means and related well to Eleanor who, by the age of ten, had lost both her parents. Roosevelt's brother would die young, too. Where Nesbitt lacked money, Roosevelt lacked close family. Through her years as the First Lady of New York and of the United States, the two maintained a close friendship.

Franklin D. Roosevelt was sworn in as President of the United States in 1932. Unemployment was surging over 25%, the United States was on the verge of economic collapse, and millions of Americans faced starvation. People had to get creative with how they fed themselves and their families. Within months of his first term as President, Roosevelt swept the country with his New Deal, which lasted from 1933 to 1939. A Civilian Conservation Corps (CCC) was created to supply jobs and rebuild infrastructure. Four million new jobs were created with the inception of the Civil Works Administration (CWA), which worked on new construction, and stability was given to older Americans with the establishment of the Social Security Administration. These programs, among the many others that made up the New Deal, sought to lift Americans out of the Great Depression, though some were more successful than others. FDR had reform on his mind at a time when the country was in crisis. So did his wife, Eleanor.

During the Roosevelts' days in the White House, guests were entertained with some of the worst food on Earth. Most presidents entertain like kings with opulence and exquisite dining. This was not part of the protocol of the Roosevelt administration. Enter Eleanor's lifelong friend, Henrietta Nesbitt. Hope is developed through the service to others. What must be recognized is that a person cannot be a great servant from a high pedestal. The 32nd President of the United States and the First Lady dined on bread and butter sandwiches and cold soups. From 1932 to 1945, the White House, the palace of the United States, was notorious for terrible dining. Guests were shocked, and it seemed like a paradox that such a magnificent building served food that was common, inexpensive, and not very well-made.

The menu at the White House may not have matched the standards established by so many administrations, but the food served paralleled the shift in the diet of so many Americans. The change can be credited to Eleanor Roosevelt and Henrietta Nesbitt. The two had an agenda. The food they served was to be an example for all cooks across the country. The simple fact was that overpriced meals were not an option for a growing population. Americans needed a total shift in mindset, and Roosevelt and Nesbitt were making it clear that even the White House would pursue that shift.

First Lady Roosevelt did not grow up poor; she was raised in upper class society. In Roosevelt's social circle, some meals consisted of enough food to feed impoverished families for weeks. Though open to conjecture, it may have been the loss of her mother and father at an early age that gave her an empathy for those who had less. She cared about people more than protocol. Since Roosevelt came from wealth, it makes sense that the kitchen and cooking were as foreign to her as a lake is to a camel. According to some accounts, scrambling eggs was the most complex cooking she understood. Though she did not have a familiarity with the kitchen, Roosevelt did understand that her example had the potential to influence a nation who desperately needed guidance during the Depression.

Like many Americans of the Depression era, Henrietta Nesbitt had fallen on hard times. Her husband was jobless, and the only money coming in was through baked goods she was selling out of their house. There were no bailouts—no billion dollar civilian rescue plans. People in need had to depend on their friends and, more importantly, themselves. That is when the phone rang at the Nesbitt house. Eleanor Roosevelt, the First Lady of the United States, called her longtime friend for a favor. She wanted her to take over as the housekeeper of the White House.

The irony is that Nesbitt had absolutely no experience in house-keeping or leading a staff, but Eleanor Roosevelt was not after experience. She wanted *reality* in the White House. The Nesbitts were struggling like most Americans. Money was tight, food was basic, and concerns were high. Roosevelt's stance was simple— the White House should not be immune. Roosevelt's first request of Nesbitt was to change the kitchen. In her memoir, Nesbitt recalled that she was shocked by the unsanitary conditions the first time she walked into the White House kitchen. More than a few eyebrows were raised when Nesbitt changed the mindset and vison of that kitchen. The push in America was to develop meals that served a healthy diet on a reasonable budget, so that would now be the standard protocol in the White House, too. The change was covered heavily by the national media, and millions of housewives took note. The simple cuisine of the White House was adopted by homes across the country. Moderation and nutri-tion replaced unnecessary spending and gluttony.

It was one thing to put out recipes and ideas that were practi-cal, but there is joy in eating. Food needs to taste good. Nesbitt's recipes just did not taste good at all. Undeterred, Nesbitt continued down her path of creating the worst tasting food in White House history. Satisfying the First Lady's agenda was one thing, but the real measure would have to be if the President and the First Lady could agree on this radical change.

President Roosevelt preferred to eat his meals at his desk while he worked. As the crippling effects of polio made him less and less mobile, he ate more and more in his workspace. Food was usually wheeled in on a simple cart. He was served his five- to ten-cent meal, just like the rest of the country. President Roosevelt could have simply lied and eaten better food while he was hidden away, but he chose not to do so. He filled his belly like the rest of the country. Regular foods that were served on this economy-driven nutritious menu were prunes, eggs, simple sandwiches, and, if you were lucky, some type of pudding for dessert. Bread and butter sandwiches were served with salmon salad, which was inexpensive at the time. Some strange experimental recipes entered the Oval Office, one of which was dried cornmeal with skim milk. Advice began spreading around Washington. "If you are invited for a meal at the White House, stuff yourself before you get there."

Laura Shapiro is a historian who writes for *The New Yorker*. In 2010, she published an article on the food in the White House during the Roosevelt administration. Her focus was not about what was served so much as why it was served. Eleanor Roosevelt, like the President, was defining her role. The First Lady wanted her kitchen to be an example for American foods and American ways of cooking them, which matched the challenges and availability of financial resources at the time. Her platform was about a change in mindset. Yes, the food was terrible, but the example the Roosevelts were setting for the country was exquisite. The message outweighed the mess. Roosevelt was trying to encourage a country to go through this together, whether each person did or did not have the means to behave or eat differently. Even when World War II began and people were faced with food rationing, the Roosevelts participated as well. The food may not have pleased the stomachs of those special few who spent time in the White House, but the example of the simple diet of the Roosevelts set a tone for the nation. They gave a country hope and purpose in a time when it would have been easy to give up. The Roosevelts did not serve by giving away money or forgiving loans, rather they set an example by the way they lived. They knew if all Americans adopted these habits, it would get the United States through a very challenging time. The Roosevelts empowered a nation of hope.

Pandemics are rare, so I will safely assume the term *social distancing* will rarely be used outside of very remote widespread disease issues. Social distancing simply means this—if illness by chance leaves my body in the form of a sneeze, you are far enough away that the illness will not affect you. On a sunny day in April, I was on a walk with my friend Rich in Mt. Hope Cemetery in Rochester, New York. He is a teacher like me. I texted him to see if he wanted to get together amidst a pandemic. We agreed to go for a walk with social distancing. After three weeks of being cooped up in my house under government-issued warnings, a walk with a friend produced a joy I had not felt in weeks. No screen or virtual world will ever replace the presence of another person. Period. I know it because I felt it.

It was Rich's choice to walk in a cemetery during a pandemic. My mind would say, *yup, death has been in the news, let us walk a stretch of beach*. I am glad we walked in Mt. Hope. This cemetery is a Victorian architectural marvel of hills, ponds, and benches.

Susan B. Anthony and Frederick Douglass are buried there. On that day, Rich and I found ourselves staring, mesmerized, at one particular stone. We were in a military section of the park, and I was trying to figure out if certain graves were Civil War Veterans or if they had fought in the Spanish-American War. Mt. Hope Cemetery is dense with headstones, however in one area a large stone surrounded by grass stands alone with a simple inscription: *The Jewish Poor Lot, Dedicated October 1885. The Rochester Jewish Community Provided for their Burial. ALL ARE EQUAL BEFORE GOD. May Their Souls be Bound Up in the Bonds of Eternal Life.*

The birth and death years on a headstone are a lot like a product creation and an expiration date. The most important part of the marker is that dash between the two dates. That dash is a person's life. The words on the memorial to the poor Jewish members of the community confirm that equality means everyone. Dignity is not reserved for those of privilege. It is the honor and a duty of those that have so much to share with those who have less. To share is a choice, but that choice has consequences. Selfishness leads to misery, but charity comes with joy for both the receiver and the giver. Those Jews of 1885 did not have to make a hallowed ground for those with less, but they did. They did not do it before or after the dates on their individual graves, but instead chose to create a space while the dash on their stone was alive. 135 years later, a stone placed by a Jewish community was reminding two men brought up as Christians a valuable lesson—*live your life so when you die the poor will mourn the loss of a friend.*

My sons, Aaron and Cory, are Eagle Scouts. I survived their Eagle Scout projects. Any parent who has traveled down the path of raising an Eagle Scout can attest that it is not easy to allow your child to make mistakes. Once, 2,000 pounds of crushed stone was supposed to be delivered to Cory's project site. The key phrase here is "supposed to be." We drove eighty miles with workers to see that the stone was not there. I nearly lost my mind. My blood pressure went up during the projects, but in the end, my sons were able to make the world a better place.

Students that are in scouts and school clubs eventually graduate or age out. Because of the time constraints, service is taught as a project or time-regulated activity. It is good to introduce the idea of serving others. However, the constraints of aging cause a misinterpretation of the word *service*. Is living a life of service about scheduling time to serve? Absolutely not. Service is a mindset. The circumstances of life dictate the intensity of service, not hours or projects. That is the real world. Schools and great organizations like Boy Scouts keep doing service. Nothing is better for the development of empathy, understanding, or togetherness. But there needs to be post-service counseling. The education that would be provided during this counseling is that though a student has completed a project or a set number of hours, in the real world, there are no boundaries to service. Service is a lifestyle, not a project. This education should start at birth.

On September 9th, 2007 came another one of my father's reflections. My father writes in spurts. The date is insignificant, and so is the way it arrived. Here is what Dad wrote:

Muttle's [my father's mother] strong feeling and compassion for people showed up in many ways. During the winter in the early 1940's, one could call the Burgermeister's office and request POWs, mostly French soldiers, to remove snow. A German soldier brought several French POWs to do the work. One was not allowed to give these POWs any food or cigarettes, etc. But, from the little we had, Muttle always found a bowl of soup, a cigarette or two and matches (strictly forbidden!) and gave them to the

Frenchmen. *Their appreciation showed up at a later time, and after our town, Sulzbach, was occupied by the French Gaullist for about a week, or ten days.*

It was a horrible time for Muttle. At one time they broke into our cellar and took the food that was stored there. They could not get into the house as the front door was heavy oak and had metal steel bars on it. The house was built in the 1630s. Shortly after the troops left, our doorbell rang. Muttle looked out from the second floor and there was a Frenchman with several jars of food (canned by Muttle), and he asked for her to open the door. Muttle was afraid to open the door, but the man said in French—he knew Muttle knew French—to open the door. Muttle went downstairs and opened the door. In came the former POW that cleared the snow. Muttle recognized his face. He put the jars, which he held in his arms, on the table and said in French, "Madam, I want to return this. Being a French soldier is a lot of shit!" With that, he made a military salute and left. Muttle's generosity toward this former POW was rewarded.

Chapter 9
Talent Has a Flat Distribution, Opportunity Does Not

"William Bradford, speaking in 1630 of the founding of the Plymouth Bay Colony, said that all great and honorable actions are accompanied with great difficulties, and both must be enterprised and overcome with answerable courage."
-President John F. Kennedy
Speaking at Rice University, September 12, 1962

- 1 -

In 1931, American freelance writer and historian James Truslow Adams wrote the book The Epic of America. He had achieved the Pulitzer Prize for History with his work, The Founding of New England. Ironically, at a time where America and most parts of the world were entrenched in the Great Depression, Adams chose optimism when he first coined the phrase "The American Dream." According to Adams, the American dream was as follows:

...that dream of a land in which life should be better and richer and fuller for everyone, with opportunity for each according to ability or achievement. It is a difficult dream for the European upper classes to interpret adequately, and too many of us ourselves have grown weary and mistrustful of it. It is not a dream of motor cars and high wage, but a dream of social order in which each man and each woman shall be able to attain to the fullest stature of which they are innately capable, and be recognized by others for what they are, regardless of the fortuitous circumstances of birth or position.

Having lived through the Roaring Twenties and the econom-

ic collapse of the 1930s, Adams wrote his work to remind people about moral value. He had grown concerned that the desire for material goods and money were interfering with the original foundation of America, which was built on "quality and spiritual values." He warned that making a living was replacing our desire to live a rich and full life. Is the American dream still alive today? It would be difficult to argue that most people do not want more money in their bank accounts, and overspending is a trend.

Lawrence Bacow's present life is as interesting now as the roots from which he came. He was born in Pontiac, Michigan to a mother who survived Auschwitz and a father who had fled anti-Semitic persecution. A young Bacow discovered a love for teaching as a sailing instructor and coupled this joy with a robust aptitude for law. He became widely regarded as an expert on non-adjudicatory approaches to conflicts as a professor for twenty-four years at the Massachusetts Institute of Technology. Surrounded by a legal system that looks for loopholes to gain an edge, Bacow worked on developing hope by advocating for compromise and understanding.

What role does education and active citizenship have on the discovery of hope and purpose? In 2001, Dr. Bacow became the president of Tufts University, and in 2018 he was inaugurated as the twenty-ninth president of Harvard University. In one generation, two poor refugees had a son who rose to the highest position at Harvard. Bacow is a real success story that grew out of an unlikely reality, and his life and philosophy will show that circumstances do not have to define destiny, hope, or purpose. Bacow has been mentored by three Nobel Prize winning economists and in 2010, he was appointed to the board of advisors for the White House Initiative on Historically Black Colleges and Universities by President Barack Obama.

ALBRECHT: I appreciate you taking the time to talk with me. As the president of Harvard, I assume that you are a busy man. Your life story is so interesting, but when I heard you run marathons and sail, both of which I love, I knew that I had to talk with you. I also read that you are an Eagle Scout. My sons are also.

BACOW: What do you sail? I've got to ask you.

ALBRECHT: I grew up on Keuka Lake, one of the Finger Lakes in up-state, New York. I taught sailing on fiberglass and wooden boats called K-Boats. They were unique to that lake. I referred to them as floating bathtubs. They are hard to tip, were not the fastest boat, and great for teaching kids. What are you sailing?

BACOW: Well, right now, we don't have a second home, but we do have a boat that is our second home, so we have a Danish boat. It is called X-yacht, a forty-foot sloop, which we sail to Maine every summer. I grew up in Michigan on inland lakes. My first boat was a Snipe. A very popular boat in the Midwest at the time was something called a Wayfarer. It is an in-proctor design, sixteen-foot, semiplaning hull. I raced those, and then I sailed collegiately for MIT, did an Olympic campaign, and used to race 470s. I was never a big-boat sailor, but now, like I say, we cruise. It is just great to spend time on the water with family.

ALBRECHT: If there is wind—sometimes we get dead wind on the Finger Lakes.

BACOW: I will always say a bad day on the water still beats a good day in the office.

ALBRECHT: As a teacher, I came to the realization that the understanding of the word *hope* is affecting the world around us. I believe the word has carried different meanings in the past, and the current interpretation of hope is affecting the way that people behave, educate, and conduct daily life. It has prompted me to seek people who can shed different light on this topic to make a better world.

BACOW: Good for you! I should tell you that my fourth-grade teacher was profoundly influential in my life. So much so, that when I became the president of Tufts, I tracked her down. I had been in touch with her all the way until I was in college and then lost touch with her. She had retired, and she had moved to Florida, so it took some sleuthing to find her. But when I became president of Tufts, I tracked her down. I not only invited her to come to my inauguration, but I invited her to come as my guest with her husband. So, we brought her up for it. What she didn't know is that in my inaugural address, I spoke about the importance of great teachers. I spoke about the great teacher in my life, and I was very fortunate. As an undergraduate, I had a mentor [Robert Solow] who took a great interest in me and went on to win the Nobel Prize in economics. He was there. My graduate school mentor [Thomas Schelling] was there. He also won the Nobel Prize in economics. I talked about them, but then I said that one of the most important teachers in my life I met long before I went to college. Shirley Chandler was my fourth-grade teacher at Webster Elementary in Pontiac, Michigan. I talked about her, then I mentioned her by name. I had her stand and be recognized. It was a magical moment, so fourth-grade teachers are very important. My undergraduate thesis advisor, Robert Engle, also won the Nobel Prize.

ALBRECHT: What was special about Mrs. Chandler?

BACOW: Well, what I said about her is that she taught me the importance of listening because other people had important things to say. She was also a great teacher in every other dimension, but I was one of these kids who had my hand up all the time. I wanted to answer every question. She literally pulled me aside and said, "You're very smart, Larry. You have the answer, but you need to let other people answer these questions. You need to listen to them because you can learn from them, too." It was a good life lesson.

ALBRECHT: Do you think that you still retain that lesson—listening?

BACOW: I try. I think I certainly changed back then and learned a lesson.

ALBRECHT: I have read about some of the creative work that you have done when navigating certain obstacles in pursuit of hope. First off, before we look at hope through your lens, how would you define yourself?

BACOW: I'm a teacher. I'm a scholar. I am an academic.

ALBRECHT: How do you see the role of a teacher?

BACOW: I spent my whole career teaching in one way or another. I fell in love with teaching. Actually, the summer after my freshman year in college, when I spent the summer teaching sailing, I realized that I really enjoyed it. I spent the next two years teaching sailing, and I went to graduate school. I didn't expect to be an academic, but I did some teaching to make money in graduate school. I was a teaching fellow for a couple of courses, and then when I was writing my dissertation, I had the chance to teach a class at Holy Cross in Worcester. I enjoyed that and then had an opportunity. I expected to go work for the federal government, but suddenly I had an opportunity to fill in for someone who was on leave for two years at MIT, and I did it, loved it, and two years turned into twenty-four years. I used to teach a variety of things. I used to teach environmental economics, environmental policy, but I am also a lawyer, so occasionally I would teach law related classes.

ALBRECHT: You are a first generation American. Would you tell me a little about your parents and how they impacted your life?

BACOW: Both my parents were immigrants. They were both refugees to this country. My father was born in Minsk and came here before the war [World War II] to escape the pogroms of Eastern Europe. My mother was born in a small farming village in Germany. Sadly, she lost her entire family in the concentration camps. She was liberated by the Russians. She was in Auschwitz, and she was not only the only member of her family to survive the war, but she was also the only Jew from her town to survive the war. She came to the United States on the second liberty ship that brought refugees from Europe after World War II. She was just nineteen years old and came here with literally a couple of suitcases. She had an aunt and uncle who had left Germany in 1936 and somehow managed to find their way to Detroit. They were her only relatives she had. She went to live with them, met my father, and got married. I have often said that *where else can you go literally from one generation from off the boat with nothing to having your son become the president of Harvard?* It is higher education that makes that possible, and so the reason that I do what I do is to ensure that future generations have hope and opportunity in the same way I enjoyed.

ALBRECHT: How did your parents instill values in you?

BACOW: Well, I think the way parents do instill values, not so much by what they say but by what they do. Their own experience made them sympathetic and empathetic toward those who were less fortunate. They realized that people had helped them, so they tried to help others. I think that I learned that from them.

ALBRECHT: I read that making and creating equal opportunity at Tufts University was a priority of yours. Was that because of the influence of your parents?

BACOW: I said in my inaugural address at Harvard that talent is flatly distributed but opportunity is not. What I meant by that is proportionately there are as many smart kids located any place in the country as there are any place else—smart kids. Those smart kids may not all have the same kind of opportunity, and so I think it is up to us to try and ensure that they get the opportunity to succeed. That's why making a great kindergarten through twelfth-grade education is really, really important. That's why making sure people have access to good college education is really, really important regardless of their ability to pay for it. That's why I was so determined to raise money for financial aid at Tufts.

ALBRECHT: Active citizenship was an educational initiative that you promoted as well. Would you elaborate on this and how it should be taught?

BACOW: I have yet to meet anyone who will say that the world is perfect. It is not a political statement. Liberals don't think that it is perfect. Conservatives don't think it is perfect. Democrats don't think it's perfect. Republicans don't think it's perfect. Nobody thinks that the world that we live in is perfect, and if you don't think it is perfect, the only way it gets better is if good people work to make it so. This is a responsibility, which I think that we all bear, and it doesn't make a difference what you do for a living. Everyone has the responsibility to make the world a better place. That requires people willing to get involved. They need to be active, willing, engaged, and effective citizens. It means that they be willing to work within their communities to strengthen their communities.

And, when I say communities, I am not just talking about where they live, although we need that. We need people to run for the school committee. We need people who are willing to volunteer for the PTA. We need people who are willing to run for public office. We need all that. We need people to inform themselves of the candidates, the issues, and vote. But we need people who are willing to get involved in all kinds of communities, whether or not they are professional communities, volunteer communities, communities of faith, and in my experience, people who tend to be leaders in one type of organization are often leaders in another. People gravitate toward those people because they see opportunity where others only see challenges. They have a way of bringing people together when others only see differences. They have the ability to see resources, where others only see scarcity. We need more people like that, and I think that the way we get them is to give people both, a sense of their responsibility—you can't sit around and wait for somebody else to go solve a problem, especially a public problem—but also to give them the tools that they need to do that. That's why I think that educational institutions have a responsibility to try to educate their students to be active, engaged, and effective citizens. We know from research that communities where people are engaged and involved, tend to be healthier communities. They tend to be stronger communities. It's that engagement. That willingness to get involved that creates social capital that allows communities to address difficult, challenging problems.

ALBRECHT: If you have generations of families that have been apathetic, how do you get those families to start engaging?

BACOW: I think partly by naming the problem. If nobody is willing to get involved, can we expect anything to get better? You know, one of your questions was *how do you define hope?* Hope is the belief that the future is going to be better than the present or the past.

ALBRECHT: So then, you would see a strong connection between active citizenship and the discovery of hope and purpose.

BACOW: Yes. If nobody is worrying about how to make the world better, if nobody is acting to do so in ways that can demonstrate to others that change is possible, then why should anybody ever have hope?

ALBRECHT: You are a lawyer. You have a law degree, but as far back as your time at MIT, you were looking at non-adjudicatory ways of resolving conflict?

BACOW: Correct.

ALBRECHT: It feels almost paradoxical for a lawyer to advocate for this. Would you elaborate on that philosophy?

BACOW: Partly, I was frustrated by what lawyers do, and that came out of going to law school. I thought too often lawyers focused on those narrow aspects of problems, which gave people leverage over certain processes—the dimensions of problems that were likely to lead to litigation, as opposed to focusing on the underlying issues that gave rise to the conflict in the first place. So, if people were upset that people wanted to, let's say, build a powerplant near them, the issue that would get framed in the lawsuit was not, or whether or not, is this a good site for the power plant or is this a bad site for the power plant? Under what conditions would it be fair to build a power plant there, given that the impact to those that live around it may be negative? Rather, the things that would get litigated were like, did the agency that built the power plant hold a proper hearing? If you built the power plant there, would the power plant affect a certain endangered species? The issues that would be litigated often were not at the heart of whether or not this is a good or a bad decision. They just gave one party or another leverage over the decision, and so, I was interested in how we could have a different conversation that went to the real issue at controversy as opposed to simply the one that provided the hook, which got people in the courthouse door. So, it is my interest in negotiated or non-adjudicatory approaches to the resolutions to disputes.

ALBRECHT: Your approach to conflict resolution parallels your belief in hope, which is to build a better future for people. Correct?

BACOW: Yes.

ALBRECHT: This is achieved, not by looking out for just yourself, but by looking out for everybody. Would you agree with that?

BACOW: Well, but also expecting people to act in certain ways. It is irrational to see people act in self-interested types of decisions. In citing disputes—where should we build power plants? Where should we build prisons? Where should we build airports? Where should we build hazardous waste facilities? Most people would acknowledge that in society there is a need to have airports, power plants, places to store and contain hazardous waste. They just would prefer that it be built someplace else, not next to them. The people who object to these things are not irrational when they complain. They would be unambiguously worse off if these things would turn up in their backyard. We make a mistake when we assume that they are being irrational, so a lot of my work went to the question of how do you address these concerns, how do you find the right location to do these things, and what does it mean for something to be the correct location? How do you compensate those people that, in some cases, might be net losers? How do you redistribute some of the benefits from these facilities from those that will benefit from it to compensate those who would be adversely affected by it?

ALBRECHT: You have traveled extensively. I have noted a trend that there is a correlation between equity and hope. What is an example of one of the finest places you have seen that promotes equity, possibly in a very creative way, in education?

BACOW: I believe that one way that we promote inequity in education, in kindergarten through twelfth education in this country is we rely far too much on the property tax to fund education. So, if you look at how kindergarten through twelfth education is funded in many other parts of the world, it's not through a property tax, so that wealthier communities are in a position to spend more on education getting to students than poor ones. Here I think that we could learn a lot from the rest of the world. We should fund kindergarten through twelfth education more equitably through a national form of taxation the way many other countries do it. In fact, we would be better off if we did it at just the state level instead of just relying on the local property taxes as much as we do. I don't know what it is like in New York, but I do know in Michigan, you could live on one side of the street and be in one school district, and that district would spend twice as much per student to educate them as the district that was located on the other side of the street.

ALBRECHT: That's true in New York, too.

BACOW: Inequity arises by the way that we finance kindergarten through twelfth education. Much of the rest of the world does not do it that way.

ALBRECHT: Is money the biggest obstacle we face in inequity in education?

BACOW: Well, I think it would be a good place to start if you wanted to start addressing the inequities that exist. Another even more radical idea that some have proposed is literally—I am not advocating this, but it is an interesting thought experiment—is if you were to eliminate private schools in kindergarten through twelfth-grade education, then those who have the resources would not be able to pull their kids out of public schools and put them in private schools. If that were the case, there would probably be a lot more political support in at least some communities to address persistent problems. I served as a town meeting member in the town I was living in—about 1981. It was one of the oldest towns demographically in Massachusetts, and it was also a town where a large percentage, because of demographics, sent their kids to parochial schools. There was very little support for public education in that town. There was little support for increasing taxes to support educational investment in kindergarten through twelfth education. It was either because people did not have kids because they were elderly or if they did, they sent them not to the public schools.

ALBRECHT: I see the same inequities in New York State, too. Your thoughts have been fascinating. Thank you for taking the time to speak with me today.

BACOW: You are welcome, and good luck with this project.

- 2 -

ESTHER HOBART MORRIS found herself in a predicament. As a Justice of the Peace, her job was to keep law and order. She took an oath when she was appointed to the position in South Pass City, Wyoming. What was once a thriving town was in decline, losing over seventy-five percent of its residents over a two-year span. Judge J.W. Stillman, who Morris had replaced, refused to hand over his court docket, and with few places to turn, she appointed her sons to the titles of district clerk and part-time deputy clerk and turned the living quarters of her sod-roofed house into a one-room court. One of her greatest opponents, John Morris, would often make such a scene in her court that she had to have him jailed. The year was 1870, and John was Judge Morris' husband.

Fifty years prior to the passage of the nineteenth amendment, Wyoming territory had already granted women the right to vote. In doing so, the Wyoming territory became the first place in the world to universally adopt the passage of women's suffrage. Why Wyoming? At the time, the state had far more men than women—a six to one ratio—and the decision was meant to entice more women to move to the territory. The Homestead Act further encouraged women to move to the territories due to its gender-neutral language. Circumstances and laws opened the door for women to hold office, but just because a law is passed does not mean that the thoughts and sentiments of the people change overnight. Esther Morris had to face opposition in public and within her own home. Outside of Wyoming territory, opposition was heavy, and this was part of the delay to grant Wyoming statehood until 1890.

One hundred and fifty years later, the United States would celebrate the 100th anniversary of women's suffrage with twenty-six women occupying the one hundred seats of the United States Senate and 106 of the 441 members of the United States House of Representatives. Though the number of women holding public office has increased with each election cycle, even in the fast-paced world of instant information, the movement to full gender equity is slow. Gender is not an obstacle, but ingrained mindsets have prevented many groups from getting their equal opportunity to sit at the table.

Dr. Bacow's story is proof of the American dream that James Truslow Adams named in 1931. Bacow's parents were poor refugees, but their son became the president of Harvard. Each person has a choice to make, and often it is made long before he or she is truly conscious of the implications. An individual's circumstances—poverty, physical challenges, ethnicity, or any of the laundry list of conditions people allow themselves to be shackled by—

do not define the capability of the character. However, parents are entirely responsible for molding the early self-perception of their children. If a child is told that they are oppressed, they will feel oppressed. Having less money and items allows for clarity on what a person *does* have.

Bacow's recollection of his parents was that of learned empathy for others. Instead of wallowing in the pity of being Jewish refugees, Bacow's parents created a path to hope by focusing on what positive aspects of their lives they had control over. This meant swallowing anger, fear, and horrific memories. In doing so, they created a formula that promoted hope. This is extraordinarily difficult to do, and it required Bacow's parents to see beyond their circumstances to identify what they wanted for others, especially their son. As Bacow defined the word, hope is making tomorrow better than today or yesterday. Like Esther Hobart Morris, Lawrence Bacow's story is one of overcoming obstacles, promoting equal opportunities for all people, and not fearing the role of leadership. All of these are key elements for the rediscovery of hope and purpose. Bacow is living proof that the American dream is still alive and well. What he did not explicitly state in his interview is the demanding schedule he holds and the long hours of work he has put into his own life to make his parents' American dream possible. It is possible to become highly successful within one generation, but it does not happen by chance.

Bacow is Harvard's president. Though Harvard is a private school, Bacow believes that a greater focus on public schools would alleviate inequity. Local taxes can vary greatly from school district to school district, so by eliminating funding through property tax, financial resources could be equally allocated between institutions of learning. This, in turn, equalizes the price per pupil from one town to the next. As Bacow pointed out, many countries already take this approach.

Bacow also asserted the value of great teachers. Nestled in his inauguration speech between two Nobel Prize winning economists was a tribute to Shirley Chandler, Bacow's fourth-grade teacher. Her advice was to listen to others. Listening guides us toward the rediscovery of hope and purpose. In chapter six, Peter Mehlman gave himself the same advice: *shut up and listen.* Whether you are the president of Harvard or the writer of iconic comedy, the path to hope involves absorbing the contributions of every person. If hope is discovered in part by listening, then this confirms that each person on this planet has something to contribute. All people have value. It is with that mindset that Bacow set forth in very few words the formula for the improvement of our communities:

If you don't think it is perfect, the only way it gets better is if good people work to make it so. This is a responsibility, which I think that we all bear, and it doesn't make a difference what you do for a living. Everyone has the responsibility to make the world a better place.

- **3** -

WHEN I WAS seven, I spent a lot of time in my neighbor's basement. He was the first kid in our town to own a video game called *Pong*. We ignored the ping pong table right behind us to play ping pong on a television screen. It was mesmerizing, and we would play it for hours. There was no color, and it only produced two sounds—one when the ball hit a player's paddle, and one when a player scored.

I was on a layover in Chicago's O'Hare airport waiting for a connecting flight to San Francisco last year. I had ninety minutes, so I took a walk. Nearly everyone was on a cellphone. Curiosity is my medicine for boredom, so out came my cellphone. I decided to walk the entire terminal—about forty numbered terminal stations. About 80% of the waiting areas had passengers sitting there. At each terminal I went into stealth mode and discretely took a picture. My science brain was at work. At the time, I was and adjunct professor teaching graduate students about education and literacy. The amount and ways people read was on my mind. On my flight from Chicago to San Francisco, I began a tally chart. There were three categories—reading a book, looking at a phone, or other. I realized on that flight, had I invested in the cellphone market around 1998, I would own the plane I was flying in. Over 75% of people were on a tablet or phone. Admittedly, some people read books on electronic devices, but the bigger point is the connection to *Pong*.

I stopped hanging out in my neighbor's basement in 1980. A friend up the street had been given an Atari 2600. WOW! Suddenly the world of *Space Invaders*, *Centipede*, and *Tank* replaced *Pong*. Removable cartridges meant that endless games would be on their way. Prior to video games, the concern over television addiction was a hot topic. Now there was another type of screen competing for people's attention. Whether in an airport or a basement, advances in technology garner a lot of attention.

In 1980, there were only a few ways to earn money. Two methods were simple—wait for Christmas or wait for a birthday. That money wasn't for fun, though; in every household I knew, that money was to be put in a savings account for college. Each Sunday, my dad gave me a quarter for my allowance. My mom taught me how to iron, and I could earn two cents for every handkerchief of my dad's that I ironed. In the summer I made a dollar for mowing our lawn and $2.50 for mowing the neighbor's. Our neighborhood was built in an old apple orchard. Each yard had knotty old green apple trees, and I made ten cents per bushel (about a hundred apples). Accumulating money was like trying to fill a gallon bucket with maple water during the dry season—it happened slowly, one drip at a time.

Pong and the Atari were houses away, and I only had boardgames. Boardgames would become analogous to the number of actual books I witnessed in Chicago's O'Hare Airport; like books, board games would soon be replaced by portable screens. The data on books was not good on that day at the airport. Only 3% of people were reading them.

I was drawn to the world of video games, so I needed to have a conversation with my parents. It was time to enter Atari world. Video games would accelerate into mainstream about the time of shopping malls. Though malls are still around today, a good Friday night as a teenager was simply walking around the mall. It was cheap and very cool. Our mall had a store named KB Toy and Hobby. Early one Saturday my dad and I went to the toy store to find out what it would cost for me to have my very own Atari. The Atari set cost $135 with tax, well over a million apples' worth. It was fall, lawn mowing season was winding down, and I had spent most of my money on baseball cards. Luckily for me, my parents were willing to negotiate. If I could earn half that amount—$67.50 still felt like an enormous amount at the time, but it was much more attainable than the full price—my parents would cover the rest. From that point on, I was checking the coin return in every phone booth.

At a young age, I was being taught a very valuable lesson, and it had nothing to do with screen addiction. My circumstances did not have to define me. In other words, the fact that I was eight years old and had no money did not mean that I could not afford the Atari set, I just would have to work for it—not on credit, but with real labor. Two cents at a time I ironed my dad's hankies, one bushel of green apples at a time, I accumulated dimes, and when the snow came, I shoveled. Eight months later, my baseball card collection had not grown, but my piggybank swelled to $67.50.

As human beings, do we have a responsibility to earn our money. What if my mom and dad just simply said, "He really wants that Atari? We should just get it. It will make him happy." Would I be the same person that I am today? I do not think so. There is a moral message to what my parents put me through—if you want something, save up and do not give up. As I grew closer and closer to that $67.50, I became proud. Pride is a cornerstone of hope and purpose. Pride does not happen by luck; it is born from grit and discipline. An old baseball coach friend of mine had a saying: "Discipline without desire is drudgery." Discipline and desire are the fertile soils that can grow the flowers of hope and purpose.

There are major differences between wants and needs. I was saving money to buy a toy. The ethic of sustained hard work has led me to be a productive adult, but I grew up having nearly all my needs met. Poverty was not a defining factor of my childhood. Is it then fair to say that a person in the most challenging of situations can rise to meet their goals? What if the Atari set was replaced with a need such as food? Is it fair to teach people to have high expectations for themselves when they have less? Do a person's circumstances and the place where their seed is planted define their entire life's work?

Benjamin Franklin was born on January 17th, 1706 in the heart of the British Colonies in Boston, Massachusetts. Most people know about Franklin's accomplishments. He helped to write both the Declaration of Independence and the Constitution, and he did so while his son was a loyalist and governor of New Jersey. He was the oldest of the Founding Fathers, and one could say, he was the father of the original United States leadership. To have the strength to face adversity later in life, he would have needed years of practice. George Washington, our first president, was forty-four when the Declaration of Independence was signed; Franklin was well past seventy. Franklin was in his eighties when the American Constitution was ratified. Not only was he able to survive the fight for independence, but he was able to overcome insurmountable odds years prior.

Franklin was the fifteenth of seventeen children. His father was a soap and candlemaker. There was no extravagance or luxury, but from an early age Franklin learned the value of sustained hard work and never losing sight of his purpose. Franklin started attending school at age eight, but by ten years old, was forced to work for his father. Most historians agree that Franklin was dyslexic, though he was one of the primary authors of two of the most important documents in American history.

Two years after leaving school, twelve-year-old Franklin began to apprentice under his older brother, James. Franklin was physically beaten by his older sibling on many occasions when he did not meet his brother's standards. Nevertheless, he would remain as a printer under the abusive supervision of his brother until 1723. In 1721, James Franklin began the publication of a somewhat successful newspaper, *The New-England Courant*. James was insistent on the quality of writing and forbid his brother to write any articles. Why would he want to write, anyway? In a parallel scenario, a similar argument may be that a paraplegic never has had the desire to run or a blind person would never want to see a sunset on a beach. Benjamin Franklin wanted to write, and he did so using the pen name, Silence Dogood. To avoid being dis-covered by his brother, he would disguise his handwriting before dropping off the letters. Eventually, however, Franklin decided to share his exploits with his brother, and he endured even more punishment. Yet, he did not leave the path of his life's purpose.

At age seventeen, Franklin left his brother. He was penniless. The act of leaving servitude was against the law, though beating a servant was not. Years later, Benjamin Franklin would write in his autobiography about the period that he was a servant to his brother. He would credit this experience as helping him under-stand one of the most important lessons of his life—that arbi-trary power should not be granted to anyone. Though a person's circumstance does not have to define them, their experiences do leave indelible marks on the lens for which they understand the world and his or her place in it. Though it can only be left to con-jecture, James' harsh treatment of Benjamin may have been one of the reasons Franklin objected so heavily to the authority of King George's tyranny over the colonies.

Instead of letting poverty control his destiny, Benjamin Frank-lin combined his talents as a printer with his tireless work ethic to pave his way into the world. Before long, he had set up his own printing press in the colonies, and his qualities of honesty, kindness, and diligence gained him a solid reputation and a lot of business. He was twenty-three when he bought a moderate-sized newspaper label, the *Pennsylvania Gazette,* and turned it into the top-selling newspaper in the area. Franklin's creativity, which had been suppressed for so long, was about to be released in an en-tirely new format—political cartoons. Franklin's freedom from his circumstances were not given to him. Like the simple lesson my parents taught me about saving money, Benjamin Franklin would define himself through his own decisions and work ethic. By age forty-two, Franklin had established the nation's first free library, founded the University of Pennsylvania, and even invented bifocals. His quote—"a penny saved is a penny earned"—would appear in a publication of his own creation, *Poor Richard's Almanack*. With this philosophy, Franklin had saved more than just a few pennies and could retire. His affluence would allow him time to transition from a businessman to a revolutionary political figure.

In the end, there is nothing that can hold back the human spirit of an individual except the individual themselves. Poverty is beatable, disabilities can be creatively overcome, and abuse does not have to control an individual years after the fact if that person truly wants a life of purpose. It is easily said but not simply done. Developing a life of hope and purpose is one of the greatest achievements a person can strive for. Great people do not obtain tremendous hope by scratching a lottery ticket. They spend years focused on their individual goals, hopes, and dreams. In some cases, even the law needs to be challenged, as was the case when Benjamin Franklin left the servantry of his brother. Each person's hopes and purposes are of equal importance, even though in the view of society, some lives are more publicly elevated than others. The truth is the most valuable life worth living is the one you hope for.

"Tell me and I forget.

Teach me and I learn.

Involve me and I remember."

- *Benjamin Franklin*

Chapter 10
Jumpman Changed the World

*"Read to your kids. It stretches their imagination a bit. It is fun,
and they feel loved while it is going on."*
-Beverly Cleary

- 1 -

*Life is corralled by those two boundaries—life and death.
There are a handful of people who are fortunate enough to defy
the odds, push the limits of their time on Earth, and grow to an
age that raises eyebrows. The extremely young and old come and
go with few wants or needs because with the furthest boundaries
of age comes simplicity. Simplicity creates clarity about the discovery of hope and purpose. As I outlined this book, I knew that I
needed to conclude with a "Yoda;" a person who had lived an extraordinary long life, worked hard, and had a clear understanding
about hope and purpose. Finding such a person is a rarity.*

*Most adults still can remember their childhood friends, the
smell of the school cafeteria, the deaths of pets, their favorite
stuffed animal, and the influence of one author—Beverly Cleary.
Whereas nowadays most kids get iTunes and Amazon gift cards,
books were the standard gifts of my childhood. Beverly Cleary entered my life on Christmas Eve of 1980 with four books:* Ramona
the Pest, Ramona the Brave, Ramona and Beezus, *and* Henry and
Ribsy.

*Cleary's novels have been a source of entertainment for chil-
dren since 1950, and her books are timeless. Driven by morals
and whimsical characters, Cleary taught kids in books like* Dear
Mr. Henshaw *that having deep feelings is a part of life. In 1984,*

this novel earned Cleary the Newbery Award. Cleary's writing help children discover hope and purpose. This iconic author has written dozens of books and sold over ninety million copies worldwide, beginning in 1950 with her first novel, <u>Henry Huggins</u>. In 1975, Mrs. Cleary was presented with the Laura Ingalls Wilder Award from the American Library Association for "substantial and lasting contributions to children's literature." In 2000, she was named a Library of Congress Living Legend in the category of writers and artists for her contributions to the cultural heritage of the United States. It is plausible that families have had four generations of readers of Beverly Cleary's stories.

Beverly Cleary is a hall of famer of children's literature. Cleary's interview happened four days after her 104th birthday. She has reached the upward boundary of life. Not everyone has the skill to capture a story in writing, but how does relating to children help them discover their hope and purpose? Does age give a person a special ability to guide people to the discovery of hope and purpose?

I was not prepared when I interviewed Mrs. Cleary. I read that she lives in Carmel, California and thought I would write to her. A quick online search provided an address and a phone number. Normally, phone numbers lead to agents. So, I called to request an interview. When a woman answered, I introduced myself and politely asked to speak to Mrs. Cleary. Getting this interview, however, would take a bit more effort on my part.

MYSTERY WOMAN: Hello?

ALBRECHT: May I speak to Mrs. Cleary?

MYSTERY WOMAN: I keep getting calls for her. Some young lady called me looking for her on Saturday. Was it you?

[Pause... just to confirm, I am a man with a deep voice. I was slightly thrown off by the suggestion that I was the *lady that called on Saturday.*]

ME: No, I am calling for the first time.

MYSTERY LADY: Are you sure you did not call on Saturday?

ME: [getting even more worried that I sound lady-like] No, I am not the lady who called on Saturday.

MYSTERY LADY: Beverly Cleary. Is she a friend of yours?

ME: No. I am a fourth-grade teacher and want to talk to her about her life and the books that she has written.

MYSTERY LADY: People keep asking about her. I never heard of her before, but I did some poking around. I think I have a number for you to call that may help. She is a writer?

ME: Wait, you don't know who Beverly Cleary is?

MYSTERY LADY: Boy, are you getting cheeky with me? Thankfully at this point I knew that she knew that I am a man... or a boy, but cheeky?

ME: I'm sorry. Beverly Cleary is possibly the greatest writer of American children's books ever. She is a very special person.

MYSTERY LADY: I hadn't heard of her until people started calling me. You are in luck. I found out where she lives. I have a phone number to give you. I am pretty sure it will help you.

ME: Thank you. This is really kind of you.

MYSTERY LADY: Have a splendid day.

I called the number that the lady gave me, again expecting a manager or an agent. All famous people have them, right? As it turns out, the answer is "no." Some people are just kindhearted people who speak for themselves. Beverly Cleary has seen 104 years of life. She was born before the First World War. When I heard the first words from Beverly Cleary's mind, I knew this was going to be a brief and one-of-a-kind interview. In so few words, she explains so much.

SELENA: Thank you for calling, this is Selena.

ALBRECHT: Hi Selena. This is Christopher Albrecht calling. May I speak to Mrs. Cleary?

SELENA: Okay, let me transfer your call. [ringing]

KATHY: Hello, health center, this is Kathy speaking.

ALBRECHT: Hello Kathy. My name is Christopher. I teach fourth grade in Brockport, New York. May I speak to Mrs. Cleary, please?

KATHY: Okay, just one moment. [long pause] Hello, Mr. Albrecht. I just went in to tell Mrs. Cleary that you want to speak with her now. I am going to transfer you to her room.

ALBRECHT: Thank you very much.

KATHY: You're welcome.

MRS. CLEARY: Hello?

ALBRECHT: Hi, Mrs. Cleary. This is Christopher Albrecht calling from Rochester, New York. How are you?

MRS. CLEARY: Well, I'm alive.

ALBRECHT: I teach fourth grade. I grew up reading your books with my mother. Now I am a teacher and have the same books I grew up with, your books, in my classroom.

MRS. CLEARY: Good! [subtle laughter]

ALBRECHT: Thank you for all the wonderful books you have written. I enjoyed every single one of them. I enjoy writing too. I am working on a book about hope and purpose. It is a book with a message for adults and children.

MRS. CLEARY: That's good because then adults won't be bored if they read it to a child.

ALBRECHT: Would you mind if I asked you some questions?

MRS. CLEARY: I guess not.

ALBRECHT: How do you define hope?

CLEARY: [long pause] I just can't think of an answer to that.

ALBRECHT: Who was your favorite teacher?

MRS. CLEARY: My second-grade teacher, who erased the horrors of my first-grade teacher and my school librarian. My second-grade teacher was Mrs. Marius. It was in Portland, Oregon.

ALBRECHT: What did you like about your second-grade teacher?

MRS. CLEARY: She let me come up, stand beside her, and read from the textbook. [subtle laughter] And she also let us bring cake at Christmas, and we had a party. [more subtle laughter]

ALBRECHT: It is amazing that you have these memories. This is over 95 years ago.

MRS. CLEARY: Oh yes, I was up there at Portland Library quite a few years ago. She came in and looked as lovely as always. [subtle laughter] I was very happy to see her. Well, she rescued a terrified little girl from the terrible horrors of the first grade.

ALBRECHT: What happened in first grade?

MRS. CLEARY: Oh, what happened? I have an affinity for her now. [subtle laughter] I didn't for many years. There were probably forty kids in the class. None of us had been to kindergarten, and I think we were a handful.

ALBRECHT: Forty kids is a lot of kids.

MRS. CLEARY: Oh, it is! [subtle laughter]

ALBRECHT: My very first chapter book was Henry and Ribsy. I read it with my mother.

MRS. CLEARY: Oh, that is just lovely. [subtle laughter]

ALBRECHT: Creativity and imagination—do you think that they are important things to teach in school?

MRS. CLEARY: Well, in my day, they tried to stamp it out. In our art class, we all had to draw this same thing and do a lot of erasing and boring things. It wasn't any fun at all.

ALBRECHT: What would you say to a teacher?

MRS. CLEARY: They should have some original ideas—I can't fully think of what I am trying to say.

ALBRECHT: Who would you say is the most creative person you have known?

MRS. CLEARY: Well, I have known quite a few creative people because we lived in Berkley. And, yes, there were many professors, and artists, generally interesting people. It was just the atmosphere. And the women seemed to have satisfied themselves, which made them interesting. [subtle laughter] Well, some women in other places were having many children in the household, and that was it. But, in Berkley there was the League of Women Voters or [laughter] something. Everybody had interests.

ALBRECHT: If you had one piece of advice for the world, what would it be?

MRS. CLEARY: Read to your kids. It stretches their imagination a bit. It is fun, and they feel loved while it is going on. I have been a children's librarian. I had a story hour once per week, but I told stories—mostly myths, or legends, or fairytales. [subtle laughter] Well, I would tell some made-up stories during the story hour, then I would read, nervously. But it got to be easy. I could read a story and then tell it in pretty much the same language, not necessarily the exact words but the same sort of language. [subtle laughter]

ALBRECHT: I have children that like to write stories. What would you tell them about how to write a story?

MRS. CLEARY: Forget writing a whole story. Write part of a story to start with. Write a description of a character, or a means to them in a neighborhood.

ALBRECHT: And it just grows from there?

MRS. CLEARY: Yes, it grows from there.

ALBRECHT: So, when you wrote all your series of books, it started with one simple story?

MRS. CLEARY: Yes. *Henry Huggins* started with a story. [subtle laughter] A worn-out mother told me, when I worked in a library, about her son bringing a stray dog home on a bus. [subtle laughter]

ALBRECHT: Was his name Henry Huggins?

MRS. CLEARY: No. I wrote the book a number of years later, but I've never forgotten that little boy and his dog, and his mother's exasperation. [subtle laughter]

ALBRECHT: That was your very first chapter book?

MRS. CLEARY: Yes.

ALBRECHT: I was told I was not a very good writer when I was young. Were you always a good writer?

MRS. CLEARY: You know, you can't always trust what teachers say to you in the lower grades. Well, the teachers always admired my imagination. We had an assignment in maybe seventh or eighth grade to write about something that took place during George Washington's war, and I made this story about a child giving his dead chicken to feed the troops, and the teacher read it and was so pleased. And all the children... I did not have to do anything more, but all of the children had to do things about—they wrote things about how they had to cook their pet pigs. I sniffed at them and said, "That is plagiarism." [subtle laughter]

ALBRECHT: Mrs. Cleary, thank you for taking the time to talk with me. I really enjoyed our conversation.

MRS. CLEARY: Me too. Well, I wish you good luck.

- 2 -

I RECORD INTERVIEWS for two reasons. Of course, I want to make sure that the transcription of the interview is accurate. More importantly, great interviews are great conversations; to have a great conversation, both people must listen. If I am worried about taking notes, I am not really listening. Listening involves hearing, but also giving consideration to each word. Though I have questions thought out prior to an interview, there is a *go with the flow* art that allows for a shared direction.

Cleary's interview was challenging, but it is a great one to listen to. Her interview had pauses that are tough to navigate over the phone. Following an interview, I listen to the conversation with headphones that amplify subtle sounds. I discovered Cleary has a very quiet laugh. When I interviewed her, I was hoping to tap into her mindset regarding imagination and hope. I wanted to know how the discovery of hope and purpose come to some people later in life. She had very little to say when I asked questions that led to abstract thought. She talked about the concrete—real stories and memories. She did not have to define hope. Cleary revealed that the glue that bonds imagination, creativity, and hope is joy. Luck and good genetics are part of the formula to living to 104 years of age, but Mrs. Cleary's subtle sounds gave clues to where the fountain of youth is located.

Cleary and I talked for about twenty minutes. There were pauses, some of which felt long. I waited through awkward silence. Brilliance emerges out of silence. What I did not hear when we were talking, but picked up later, is that she softly laughed at almost every memory, like each reflection had an ability to tickle her. At 104 years old, Cleary found joy in reminiscing in snippets. In Cleary's books, main characters are adventurous, a little naughty, and—like most children—do things that put gray hair on their parents' heads. When she talked about a worn out mother and a rambunctious son, her inflection and slight laugh weren't about writing. She had kept that memory for so long because it was about her seeing the joy of a boy and his newfound best friend, a stray dog. Nearly everything, even her reference to the horrors of first grade, were followed with a pause and laugh. Memories define our current reaction consciously and subconsciously.

How should we be living our lives? I look at my fourth graders, my own children who are in their twenties, my wife and I, and people that are still alive from my parents' generation—nearly everyone has days where they move nonstop from morning until night. There are scheduled breaks that most people work straight through. If there is something that we can get away with eliminating, we do. How much time is allotted in the days of children and adults to imagine and create for a sustained period? There is a lot of talk about the health benefits of eating correctly, exercise, and the quality of sleep. They all promote a healthy lifestyle, but what is the effect of not allowing time for daydreaming, imagining, and simple play? When a person imagines, they develop a world of limitless possibilities. If we never stop to take a look in the mirror and imagine, we never will discover why each of us is here in the first place. The recommendation straight from Cleary is teachers need to have original ideas. At that moment, we were talking about schools, but I would guess that Cleary would say all people need to imagine in their place of work, too.

When schools and communities are not mirrors of each other, mixed messages cloud the path of hope and purpose. In 2018, I visited the Googleplex in San Francisco, California. The company is constantly redefining how to create a productive work environment. Google spends money and a lot of effort on developing an environment where joy and simplicity are developed. Since hope and purpose are developed by both, Google has made the connection that hopeful and purposeful employees increase the company's success. Google employees enjoy free breakfast, lunch, and dinner. The organic food is prepared each day by a chef. They have doctors, dentists, dry cleaning, and even a massage parlor. They offer haircuts, nap pods, gyms, games, and swimming pools all on site. The discovery of hope and purpose comes with simplicity. Employee retention in a highly competitive environment like Silicon Valley means that employees have a greater sense of investment in their work, so less money is spent on recruiting talent. All of this justifies the expenditure of a re-imagined workspace. Google does not shoot from the hip. The company's department of Human Operations is constantly experimenting with everything from table size to the training current employees receive for welcoming new hires.

Are all people creative by nature? No. By temperament, some people are born more creative than others. However, the development and rediscovery of hope does not happen in a moment, and if everyone has a right to rediscover it, then it is possible for everyone to find their creative mind. Google illustrates that a space can be creative to allow simplicity and creativity while maximizing the work people accomplish.

Nobody has ever said life is fair. Some things take more work for some people than others, but hope is not about glorifying what a person has; it is about the pursuit of purpose. That aspiration is an essential part of a daily routine that needs to be developed over a lifetime and must be embedded in a person's lifestyle. If a person wants hope, they need to embrace the struggle. Some people are creative by nature, but that does not mean that a person cannot be nurtured to develop their creativity. Hope takes work, coupled with dedicated effort.

Lucas was a handful. He was in my class, and though I will never admit to enjoying a student being sick from school for a day, Lucas's perfect attendance added a gray hair or two. By the second week of school, the honeymoon period was over, and he was living up to his third-grade reputation. He swore, was sneaky, and short. Even at his size, kids were nervous around him. Lucas just would not do homework. Consequences failed. Calls home failed. Firm discussions in the hall failed. Our instinct is that by holding students accountable, they will respond. Those that do have hope. But a student that does not see purpose in themself or the world around them behaves like Lucas. One, two, or even three steps need to be taken backward before any steps are going to be made forward.

Each week, every student must stand in front of my class and present a current event. Call me old school, but I still instruct students on posture, looking up from a paper when presenting, and the use of eye contact. There is value in instructing behaviors that will never be outdated, but new school has me adding the next generation of instruction. Technology is a tool, no different than a pencil or a box of crayons. Many students develop motivation when finding their articles online because they incorporate video media and pictures into their presentations. Current events are a high point of the day because curiosity drives the dialogue between children. Children synthesize ideas and ask each other's opinions. Often, I say nothing. When Lucas was with me, I sat next to him during current events for many reasons. On top of turning my hair gray, Lucas was a doodler. You know the type—the ones that the teacher is always telling, "Stop drawing on your work."

Imagination comes in all different forms. Sometime in February, a student presented a current event about the first Mars rover. I was learning about this new world right along with the class. Lucas looked up when he saw the photographs. It was the first time he ever raised his hand. He participated, but he usually just talked right over the top of everyone. I do not remember what he asked. The content of his question is irrelevant. His actions are what drive the rest of this story. What was of value was that Lucas was fascinated by the idea of rockets. He wanted to know how far away Mars was, how the rockets got the rover there, and so on.

Teaching is a lot like putting a jigsaw puzzle together. Inspiration is analogous to attaching two adjoining pieces of a puzzle. Satisfaction comes when two pieces finally fit. People sit for hours doing puzzles because the concept of a jigsaw puzzle is akin to gluing a broken bottle back together. I found a connecting piece to Lucas's jigsaw puzzle of learning that day; he was fascinated by space and rockets.

I bought a sketch pad. It became Lucas's doodle space, and he drew rockets for a week. It grew old. I spent my own money on space and rocket books trying to inspire Lucas to read. Nope! What I was experiencing was a lot like trying to fit the pieces of a puzzle together that looked like they should fit. I was not finding the perfect match, and I found myself scratching my head.

One day after school, I walked down to the cafeteria. We have glass windows that look out to the playground. I was going to set up for the yearly spelling bee, and there was Lucas out in the snow, alone on the playground. Lucas walked to and from school because he lived in the neighboring apartment complex, but my guess is that he did not always go straight home. I never considered just how close he lived to school. I opened the door, yelled hello out to the playground, and the kid who I prayed would just be sick (I did not say that), suddenly was in the cafeteria setting up chairs. That day was the first time Lucas ever did his homework. Why? I called his mom to tell her where he was. Her response was that of relief but not because he was safe. I sensed that she needed a break, too. Lucas did his homework with me. He gave me no trouble—nothing. Right before we did the work, we talked about rockets. At that point I found two pieces of the puzzle that fit. Lucas's puzzle was at least a thousand pieces in size. There was a lot of work still to be done.

As a kid, I built rockets with my father from kits made by the Estes model rocket company. The rocket kits were constructed by gluing balsa wood fins on a cardboard roll. There was a plastic nose cone and a parachute, and some of these rockets reached an elevation of 3,000 feet. They could only be launched on calm days. Wind would be their demise. I started talking with Lucas about how my dad and I built rockets. All Lucas cared about was how to get a kit. A few more pieces of Lucas's puzzle were connected.

The thing is, up to that point, I do not believe that Lucas had ever worked for a productive and sustained time at anything. Building a rocket gave him hope and purpose because it took patience, time, and anticipation. The first light of sunrise finally gleamed in Lucas's path towards the discovery of hope and purpose. I made arrangements with his home, though I made it clear that this was no free ticket. Lucas stayed after school with me frequently. If he was going to stay, I needed to build Lucas's level of hope and purpose. If this was going to be achieved, Lucas was going to have to be held to an expectation. He did not know it, but my goal was not to have him get his homework done. I was not after a dramatic jump in his reading, writing, or math proficiency. Those would all be icing on the cake. What I was doing was looking to connect more puzzle pieces in Lucas's life. If we were going to climb academic mountains, he would have to discover hope and purpose first. I usually stay after school late, so it really was no change in my schedule. Each day, we worked together to straighten up the room, put out morning work, and get his homework done. I corrected papers and answered his questions, but often we just worked side by side in silence. Then, we built rockets.

When Lucas launched his first rocket, the Alpha, it went over a half of a mile into the sky. Lucas was in shock, and I was too. Lucas was blown out of the water by the force and intensity of seeing a rocket go clear out of sight. Me—I had already seen a rocket launch. For the first time, I witnessed Lucas finding his hope and purpose.

Beverly Cleary hit the nail on the head. Teachers need to be creative. And yes Mrs. Cleary, reading to kids makes them feel loved—so does spending quality time with them, acknowledging a child's interest, and giving each student an opportunity to serve. About the end of March was when I began hoping that Lucas would keep up that perfect attendance, but one school year is not a lifetime. It will be up to Lucas to continue down the path where he discovers his hope and purpose. In the end he will oversee his own destiny.

- 3 -

ALBERT EINSTEIN DIED in 1955. If he had lived to 1962, I imagine that he would have laughed. Deep in the technology labs of the Massachusetts Institute of Technology (MIT), five scientists were working tirelessly on a new and imaginative technology that was about to change the world, affect people's habits, and create some obsessions. It was the Cold War era, and most technological advances were driven by the military and the newly-formed, government-funded space organization—NASA.

However, these five men, all with different roles, were heavy at work on their revolutionary DEC PDP-1 computer. The scientists—Steve Russell, Martin Graetz, Wayne Wiitanen, Bob Saunders, and Steve Piner—were all trying to solve the problem of how to conquer the universe. What they were watching on the screen of their computer was groundbreaking. Two enemy spaceships, the Needle and the Wedge, were circling each other on a black and white screen. The Needle suddenly accelerated to the left and fired a silent missile at the other ship. The missile missed, but on a counterattack, the Wedge made a quick pivot, fired, and erased the Needle from the screen. The universe was conquered!

Russell, Graetz, Wiitanen, Sauders, and Piner created one of the very first video games. The citizens of the United States were bracing themselves for the escalation of the Vietnam War, and underlying fear of total nuclear annihilation was growing as the Cold War dragged on. The fight for equal rights was getting more intense every day. Yet these five men somehow escaped that reality, even if it was only for a short time. They created their own war in the "kudge room" of the MIT Electrical Engineering Department in September of 1961. The screen they were using was monochrome and looked more like navy radar than television. While the world was facing the reality of chaos, these five men were creating imagined chaos.

This new game, named *Spacewar!,* was one of the world's first video games. The programmers added stars, gravity, and hyperspace to immerse players. The influence of *Spacewar!* put pressure on other game manufacturers to make the setting of their games outer space as well. No doubt the space race President Kennedy had ignited with the Soviets had made outer space an ideal setting for the general population. Later games such as *Asteroids* and *Space Invaders,* which would hit mainstream in the late 1970s, trace their inspiration of their setting and imagination to *Spacewar!*. In 1962, when *Spacewar!* was introduced to the public, it was an instant hit.

Though the first video games were made by researchers, programmers around the world only refer to one person with the nickname of *god*—Shigeru Miyamoto. Shigeru Miyamoto would most likely agree with Albert Einstein's mindset regarding creativity. His company's history and his own imagination are models of inspiration. For most people Nintendo has been a standard presence in the electronic gaming industry. Its roots trace back to 1898, where the company got its start making playing cards. Around the middle of the twentieth century, Nintendo began branching out from card production to appeal to an audience outside of Japan. The company experimented with everything from instant rice to a taxi service. During the 1950s and 60s, they tried to manufacture novel toys that were on the cutting edge of technology. If something was there to invent, Nintendo was interested. In the early 1970s, Nintendo entered the highly competitive gaming market. Solid vision and a unique approach to being imaginative in a computerized world of binary code allowed Nintendo to come out on top at the advent of the gaming revolution.

Shigeru Miyamoto is iconic in the history of video games. Not only did he invent the *Legend of Zelda,* but he is also responsible for creating *Mario Bros.* and *Donkey Kong.* The first-generation gaming console era lasted from 1972 to 1984; the systems hooked up to a television, and most were monochrome. Miyamoto was hired by Nintendo in 1977. His first job was to create the casings for the game systems, but he soon began programming. At the time, hundreds of companies were vying for the hundreds of millions of dollars that were projected in the gaming market. The money, competition, fame, and wealth were not Miyamoto's driving force. He was successful because he removed these distractions to focus on what truly interested him—imagination. By channeling his passion, Miyamoto had hope and thus has created a legacy that remains in the gaming industry to this day.

With all of this fame, Shigeru Miyamoto lives a very simple life. Like Einstein, he sees the world as a creative place and does his best to preserve that. When Nintendo hired him, the president of the company was impressed with Miyamoto's untrained artistic skills, not his programming ability. After creating some of the world's most recognizable video games, Miyamoto was offered hundreds of highly lucrative jobs, which would have made him incredibly wealthy. He stuck with Nintendo. Why? Nintendo maintained a philosophy of pursuing innovation and happiness, carrying out the spirit of the entertainment industry with novel innovations, and constantly introducing new products beyond imagination. There is nothing in this philosophy that gets in the way of a person who values imagination. With all his notoriety, Miyamoto rides a bicycle to work and insists on not receiving a greater salary than other developers at Nintendo. Greed does not cloud Miyamoto's hope and purpose.

Traditional video games, especially those that were developed in the 1970s and 80s, were uniformly focused on accumulating points. Miyamoto grew up in a very rural town northwest of Kyoto, Japan. As a young boy, his parents allowed him to roam the natural areas surrounding his home. At one point, young Miyamoto found a cave. For days he was scared to enter it, but he eventually worked up the courage to explore. These impressionable experiences are what inspired *The Legend of Zelda*. Over fifty-two million copies have been sold worldwide. Those that have played the game will note that imagination, not points, are most valued. *The Legend of Zelda* and the games in the *Mario Bros.* franchise do keep a point value, but the focus is more about the quest. Each time a player starts, the hope is to get further in the journey. Every game in the series is about a sense of wonder and exploration, especially in open-world games. The main character, Link, serves as a protagonist in a hybrid game, which crosses storytelling and gaming. The player is frequently rewarded with helpful items or increased abilities for solving puzzles or exploring hidden areas. The deviation *The Legend of Zelda* brings to the gaming experience allows the joy of the process of gaming to shine and does not focus on the product of points. Hope is discovered by the gamer through discovery, creative thought, and experimentation. Between 1986 and 2020, nineteen different quests have been created.

Miyamoto's first success came with the *Donkey Kong* arcade game. A fan of Popeye the Sailor Man, he understood the appeal of a twisted love triangle much like that of Popeye, Bluto, and Olive Oyl. When *Donkey Kong* was conceived, Bluto became the ape, and the carpenter and the girl were mirror reflections of Popeye and Olive Oyl. The idea of using catapults and seesaws proved too difficult for the programming team, so Miyamoto proposed a four-level system where the carpenter would have to dodge barrels. The programming was much simpler because the character repeated his actions on all four levels. When the game was sent to America for test marketing, it was rejected. The game was just too different from the shooting games of the time.

Despite this, *Donkey Kong* was an instant success. Most of Miyamoto's games were successful. Jumpman was eventually renamed Mario, after Mario Segale, Nintendo's warehouse landlord in North America. The woman being rescued was named Polly, after the wife of a Nintendo warehouse manager, Don James. The company was small prior to the release of these games, particularly outside of Japan, and few people realized just how iconic Nintendo would become.

Imagination is the fundamental practice of Shigeru Miyamoto. Imagination gives him hope and purpose. How, in the rapidly evolving world of game systems, was he able to remain a hopeful person? Imaginative people find inspiration in nearly everything, do not stop questioning, and are not afraid to fail. Remember, Miyamoto's ideas when developing *Donkey Kong* were too complex for the programmers of the time. He did not let that stop him from creating. Programmers probably did not know what to make of him. He did not let scientific limits stifle his creativity and acted before he thought. Had he spent too much time thinking, he may have been hampered by the limitations of the programmers. Miyamoto stayed true to being an independent thinker, even when the sales managers balked at *Donkey Kong*. In doing so, he invented an entirely new genre of video games that remains popular to this day—the platformer.

Hope takes courage and a free spirit that is not bridled by others. People with strong imaginations can face ridicule because they live outside of the box. Teachers remind students to stop daydreaming or doodling. Part of school is about learning to build the capacity for attention. It is polite to look at a person giving instruction, and often when a person is in Neverland, they miss topics in a lesson. However, do we allow students at school or adults in the workplace to spend a scheduled amount of time simply imagining? Is there time allowed in every person's day to picture ideas that may not be concrete or even have merit? What if companies, colleges, public schools, and society collectively removed roadblocks and devoted some time to imagination and creativity?

Albert Einstein acknowledged that knowledge would get you somewhere—from point A to point B—but creativity's potential destinations are infinite. If we are to rediscover hope within ourselves, we need to go back to asking questions about our children. There are no laws against playing or imagining, only people who will feel compelled to make you feel different or strange. There are times where companies, schools, or communities will say that there is no time to get creative because their agenda matters more. Will their agenda ever improve if imagination is not part of the rediscovery of hope?

In my classroom, I have an iconic poster of Albert Einstein. He is smiling and sticking his tongue out. Is it possible that Einstein was both brilliant and funny? In 1931, Einstein released the book, <u>Cosmic Religion and Other Opinions and Aphorisms</u>. Though many brilliant words were uttered by Einstein, perhaps more than any other person in history, in this book Einstein made a rather paradoxical statement: "Imagination is more important than knowledge. Knowledge is limited. Imagination encircles the world."

There is a lot of great children's literature on the market. Hollywood reads children's books too. Often, a great book will end up making its way to the big screen. It is so easy to rent the movie and so much more time-consuming to read the book. Why bother to read the book at all? Why have teachers begged students for decades to *read the book first*? Imagination is more important than knowledge. Einstein said it himself. When we read a book, we imagine the characters, the plot, and the setting. It is not possible for even a gifted novelist to paint the exact same picture in every single person's mind. Reading literature enhances the creative mind.

Hollywood is important, and a good movie is worth watching. When a movie is watched, however, you do not imagine what a character looks like, the clothes they wear, or the sound of their voice. It is told to you. Watching a movie is akin to knowledge. The sounds and the scenes are put right there in front of the audience. The creative mind is put on the shelf. In a book, on the other hand, readers are completely engaged in every sense of the word. And, if the saying that "a picture is worth a thousand words" is true, no author could fully describe a story in under a few million words. Readers get to imagine, and as Einstein said, "Imagination is more important than knowledge." Each person is unique, and the discovery of hope and purpose can be found on infinite paths. What is yours? It is up to all of us to discover hope and purpose through our mindsets, actions, the company we keep, and a little luck.

Tribute

During the final stages of the publication process, Mrs. Beverly Cleary passed away. Her timeless books have been loved by generations of young readers. It was a pleasure to work on this chapter with her. In her honor, the rest of this page is blank as a pause for all to remember a truly beautiful person.

Chapter 11
Coming to America

"The New York City skyline was another spectacular sight— very impressive—the Empire State Building and all of the skyscrapers—I still remember it well. All future arrivals into New York City were not as breathtaking as this one."
-Werner Albrecht

- 1 -

A LEAP OF faith is the path to hope and purpose for a pioneer. The discovery of hope and purpose, for most, has been traveled by people before them, and the history of the journey inspires the next person to go the same direction. Like toppling dominoes, hope causes others to see the light and follow their dreams. But there are trailblazers, too. The most unique and groundbreaking paths to hope and purpose head through uncharted waters. Those people who have the courage to break rules or barriers, face naysayers, are not afraid to fail, and trust themselves cause the world to move in a unique direction for better or for worse. Had the Wright brothers never questioned the calculations of highly-regarded mathematician Otto Lilienthal, they would have never achieved mechanically powered flight. They removed the barrier of questioning themselves and found Lilienthal's calculations to be incorrect. If Martin Cooper listened to all those who said that only wires could carry a phone network, cell phones would not have been invented in 1973. The purpose of education is to unleash the human spirit so it can travel down the path it was meant to go. Like forest leaves, each person has a time that they will change and drop, and where each one lands is unique.

When a person responsibly has full freedom of their own creativity, original thought becomes the next frontier.

On March 22nd, 1900, Anne Rainsford French Bush was the first woman to be issued a driver's license for an automobile in America. The City of Washington, D.C. issued her a Steam Engineer's License, a very progressive move since the United States was still two decades away from the passage of the 19th amendment. Bush's story was captured in the September 9th, 1952 issue of *Life* magazine. Bush was born into the high society of Washington; her father had been a friend of Abraham Lincoln. He despised horses because of their unpredictability and therefore was interested in cars. With her family's status and her father's interest in cars, Bush had no problem obtaining a license. Without opposition, the path to being a pioneer can be easy, though Bush gave up driving in 1903. The same year Bush was turning in her keys, Mary Anderson, a rancher, invented windshield wipers that were controlled from inside the car. By 1916, they were standard on most vehicles.

Sally Robinson was four-foot, eleven-inches tall and weighed eighty-eight pounds. She was twenty-seven years old and had been illegally riding motorcycles all over Washington, DC for almost a decade. The year was 1937, and Robinson had decided to get a motorcycle permit. No woman had ever tried to obtain a license to drive a motorcycle, and the police were not interested in giving one to Robinson. Though driving a car was fully acceptable, the idea of women driving motorcycles was written off until Robinson decided it was her hope and passion to be a fully licensed motorcycle operator. Her fame and pioneering effort would have been lost in the black hole of obscurity if the *Washington Post* had not captured the story on September 11th, 1937.

The roads had been open to female automobilists for thirty-seven years. Though Robinson had been riding motorcycles for recreation on and off for nearly ten years, she had been doing so illegally. She felt she was entitled to the same privileges as a man—to hold a license to operate and drive a motorcycle in public. Do a person's circumstances have to define them? In Robinson's mind, the answer was definitely *no*. Multiple obstacles were in her way; she was petite even on the smallest bikes, no female had ever attempted to obtain a motorcycle license, and the bias of the police, who issued the permits, was not in her favor. Sometimes, the only way to achieve the hope and purpose that every person on this planet is entitled to is through grit, determination, and—in Robinson's case—putting up a fight.

Robinson believed in herself. On her first examination, she achieved an eighty percent grade, and on a later exam she was well within the passing range with a ninety-two. The passing grades were not enough for the officer in charge of the exam, so she got a lawyer. With the presence of a lawyer, Robinson was allowed a road test. Unlike cars, the only way to ride along with a person on a motorcycle is by sidecar. With the lawyer no longer present, the examiner refused to sit in a sidecar out of fear for his life. It was an excuse. Robinson's persistence allowed for a road test, but due to her size, she could not kickstart the testing bike the same way that she would kickstart her own. At that point, Robinson decided to take matters into her own hands. As written in the *Post*, Miss Robinson stated, "I started cussing him out. I called him such names—well, I was ashamed of myself. But it worked, and I have the permit."

In 1937, the smallest road bike weighed over 300 pounds, nearly four times Robinson's weight. At stops, her bike would sometimes fall over. She was a small person. There was no changing that. Does the discovery of hope and purpose justify a fight or even war? That depends on the timing. Early confrontation is hard to avoid when people are passionate about their purpose in life because the human spirit is filled with emotion. Still, it should be approached with caution. The results of aggressive actions may create more obstacles than progress, but after a certain point there is often no alternative. Robinson's example shows us that there can come a point where bold action is necessary. Leaving a place of comfort can be part of the discovery of hope and purpose, and it is often the mindset of comfort that pioneering people must overcome.

My father came to America in 1959. His journey to the United States is, in all senses of the word, one of hope. He lived through the occupation of Germany by American forces during the Second World War. The Americans had left a lifelong positive example in his mind, and with an opportunity at hand, he made a decision. He was the pioneer of his family, the first to dare to travel to the United States of America. He did not have the fiery nature of Sally Robinson or the affluence of Anne Bush, but when he boarded a plane in Switzerland, he became the first in his family to head across the Atlantic. In 2011, with no occasion attached, he gave me this narrative, along with his original Pan Am 707 boarding pass.

- 2 -

Coming to America
By Werner August Albrecht

THE YEAR WAS 1959, and for a few years, I had been working for the Seiler family in Switzerland- first as controller for two hotels up in the mountains between the Furka and Grimsel passes, very close to the glacier where the river Rhone originates. One was the Hotel Belvedere and the other, the main hotel, the Glacier du Rhone. After the hotels closed for the season, I went to Zurich and was the controller for the Restaurant Ermitage in Kuesnacht-Zurich and for the Restaurant Ermitage in Berne. All of these places were owned by the Seiler family.

In those days, in order to further your career, a young fellow had to switch workplaces frequently, about every two to three years. This was considered a positive move, for you gained experience. Among other duties, one of my jobs in Zurich was to hire the staff for the restaurant, while Berne had its own management, my job was less.

At the beginning of the 1959 season, or perhaps a little earlier in 1958, I had hired Peter Bruhn as a second maître d'hotel. He was good at his position, well-liked, and knew his business. One day he came to me in the morning and told me that the night before he met an American in the restaurant. This fellow was looking for some maître d'hotel for a sizeable and fairly new restaurant just north of New York City. We talked about it and decided to mail him our resumes to his restaurant in Williamstown, Massachusetts. Well, I couldn't even pronounce Massachusetts—that is quite a difficult word for a European. Peter spoke limited English, so I made both of our resumes and letters. It did not take long, and we had a response that this man wanted both of us. We wanted to go for two, max three years—basically to see what America was like.

We told our decision to Dr. Edouard Seiler, the main owner of the Zurich and Berne restaurants. He was also part owner of a motel and restaurant near the Toronto airport. His answer was, "Why didn't you tell me this before? I could have arranged that you come to Canada." To make it brief, Peter changed his mind and went to Canada. I decided to stick with my original decision to go to the United States.

To get an immigration visa was no big problem. In those days, the United States had yearly immigration quotas for individual countries. Quotas for "developed countries", such as Switzerland, Germany, England, etc. were high and never completely filled, while quotas for less developed countries were always full. Some people had to wait for years to get their visas. I was asked to supply a tremendous amount of paperwork to the United States consulate. One of the documents was a chest x-ray. There was a problem with my x-ray. It showed scars, indicating that I had or had once had tuberculosis. I was upset and went to my doctor in Zurich since I knew that I never had TB. Dr. Barbe said that it was impossible and x-rayed me again. He told me that most people have some scarring on their lungs, and that it was possible that at one time or another I had TB to some degree. It ended up that I had to submit sliced pictures of my lungs to show that it was really of no consequence.

Harold Reder, my future American employer, mailed me a ticket from Zurich to New York. I made a visit to Edelfingen [where my father's parents lived], went back to Zurich, where Gerhard [his brother] was... or possibly he came to London from Liverpool, or maybe it was Manchester, where he taught at the university. We spent a couple days together and saw Beethoven's Ninth at the Royal Festival Hall—what a wonderful sendoff. I boarded one of the first PanAm 707 flights across the Atlantic. Up to this point, most of the aircraft traveling over the Atlantic were Constellation. The impressions were just overwhelming.

After a few hours in the air, we flew over Greenland and saw icebergs floating in the Atlantic. And it was December 2, 1959 when I had my first glance of the United States. A nice lady sitting next to me found out—I was always talking, that this was my first trip to the United States. We came from north to south along the Hudson River. In those days there was the Reserve Fleet, also known as the Moth Fleet, anchored in the Hudson. They were all of the old war ships, as I recall. It was almost time for sunset, a beautiful and clear afternoon. The New York City skyline was another spectacular sight—very impressive—the Empire State Building and all of the skyscrapers—I still remember it well. All future arrivals into New York City were not as breathtaking as this one.

Harold Reder welcomed me at Idlewood Airport [now known as John F. Kennedy International]. I was dead tired, did not feel too well, and he took me to the Motel on the Mountain. It was a Japanese style motel with a sizeable restaurant, the Restaurant on the Mountain. It was located on top of Rattlesnake Mountain, about 300 feet above the New York State Thruway near Suffern, New York. Reder also owned the 1896 House in Williamstown, Massachusetts. He leased the Restaurant on the Mountain. It was built in 1957 by an architect "imported" from Japan, Junzo Yoshimura. It was something I had never seen before. We stayed there overnight and left for Williamstown the next morning. I knew that I would return to Suffern in the near future.

The next weeks, I was living in Reder's house, and after that, in a small room at the 1896 House. You know, I couldn't get over the different architecture of the regular homes—the houses constructed of wood and drywall—so different from the ones in Europe. Many colors: blue, yellow, green, white—I never saw this before. I remember writing Muttle and Vatle [his mother and father] about it. And I took pictures with the old Zeiss Ikon camera.

I liked the town. At the restaurant, I did all kinds of jobs. I think that Reder was proud to have "imported" someone, because he showed me off to all his friends. They all wanted me to cook crepes suzette at their tables.

Soon enough, I discovered that one needs a car if I wanted to go anywhere. In Germany and Switzerland, we were walking or took the train. America was different. I needed a car. One of the bartenders talked me into buying his old Studebaker, though I don't remember what year it was, maybe from the early fifties. It was a two-seater, black with a bullet nose. I liked and bought it for $150. I had to pass a new driver's license test. Back in those days there were two different types of licenses: A license for automatic shift cars and another one for stick shift cars combined with automatic. Since I wanted to drive all kinds of cars, I borrowed one of Reder's Renaults with a stick shift, of course. Gasoline was twenty cents per gallon, or maybe even less, in those days. I did not make much money, the car was paid for (from the few dollars I brought from Switzerland), but at least I could cruise around.

It wasn't long before I was transferred to the Restaurant on the Mountain in Suffern as maître d'hotel. Suffern was interesting. I had to find myself a room—and found a neat one with a separate entrance, a quiet area and surrounded by large, parklike properties. The restaurant was a very, very busy place. The new Tappan Zee Bridge had just been completed, and it made it easier for people from New York City, West Chester County and Connecticut to come and see this unusual place, which received large amounts of its publicity because of its novelty. On a Saturday evening, it was not unusual that guests waited ninety minutes to two hours to be seated at a table. We were exhausted at the end of each night. But there was always time to go out afterward, and boy we did do it! Today, when I think back, it seems almost impossible—but we did it. For a while I had a girlfriend in New Jersey, and sometimes I went to see her after work. I drove down there and back, got a short time to sleep, then, back to work.

There came a day when Harold Reder asked me if I knew a chef who would like to come to the United States and run the kitchen of the Restaurant on the Mountain. Leopold Schaeli once was the chef at the Ermitage near Zurich—a first class chef, I don't know anyone who knows more about culinary art. I was aware that he had left Switzerland and was working in Izmir, Turkey. I wrote him, and his immediate reply was that he would come. He applied for an expedited visa. Leo was in Suffern a few weeks or months later. A room next to mine was available. That room became his.

After the Studebaker failed, I bought a Ford station wagon—8 cylinders, 1956, and extremely powerful. It probably used a lot of gas but no problem. Gas was cheap. Leo needed a car, and we found a white Mercury convertible—quite classy. One night, Leo almost lost his car. A tornado came across Long Island and headed directly toward Suffern, a rare occasion. The next morning a tree with about a ten-inch trunk laid next to Leo's car. There were just a few small scratches from the branches. He was lucky.

Over the years there were interesting people at the restaurant. Colonel Rudolf Abel, the Russian spy, was one. We did not realize, nor did any one of us know, who he was at the time. We found out after he was arrested. In 1962, he was exchanged at a bridge in Berlin for Francis Gary Powers, the American spy who flew the U2 plane that was shot down over Russia. Another visitor was Norman Rockwell. He was already old at the time. Muttle [his mother] liked his art very much. Allen Funt, the producer of the television show "Candid Camera", was a regular. Also, Danny Kaye, a well-known actor, singer, dancer, and comedian was there frequently. It's impossible to name them all.

One day I met the athletic director of the Army Academy at West Point. He was a colonel. He was a very pleasant man, and he invited me up to West Point. I took him up on it and visited him at *The Point.* He gave me a special tour. What a place!

I remember the Sunday in November when Oswald, the JFK assassin, was shot and killed by Jack Ruby. I heard the news on the radio, while driving to work, and when I arrived, the restaurant was extremely busy. People were glued to the television in the lobby, while waiting to be seated. I had briefly stopped to watch this too. So did Ricky, the then maître d' (by then I was promoted to assistant manager). A waitress came to Ricky and told him that a couple wanted a certain bottle of wine. Ricky went to the table and said that Lee Oswald was shot and probably killed. The lady jumped up from her seat and said, "Lee? Lee was shot?" She was quite hysterical. The man who was with her took her by the arm and said, "Let's go." So, they left. After a while, Ricky came to me and told me the story. I asked him if he followed them to get a license plate number—he did not. Later in the afternoon came the head hostess Helen's husband to pick her up from work. He was the chief of police in Hilburn, a small town at the bottom of the mountain—with a one-man police force. I told him the story, but there was nothing we could do at this point. We found out weeks later that Oswald was raised in the Bronx, and we made the assumption that this woman was probably also brought up in the Bronx and knew Oswald.

But the most interesting person for me was Mr. Lewis. I don't remember his first name. He was a lawyer in Suffern. After World War II, he was a lawyer for the prosecution of the Nuremburg trials. In contrast to many other Jewish people, he understood how things happened in Germany during the Hitler era. He was not one who carried a grudge. He took me into his office and showed me pictures of the trial—it was fascinating.

Other people were different. People would ask me where I was from. My accent in those years was stronger than it is today. My answer was Germany. Now, most Jewish people continued to be friendly. There were others. It wasn't a small amount. No open hostility, but more or less, we want nothing to do with you! I thought that I should be smarter and avoid situations as such. Therefore, I said, "I come from Switzerland." It wasn't a direct lie. I came from working in Switzerland. I never pretended to be Swiss, although it wouldn't have made any difference. Others, still having the number tattooed on the inside of their forearm, were just outstanding and wonderful people. But this point in history is now over. Thank God.

To go along with this, I experienced a situation, which was insignificant, but really troubled me. One Monday morning, my day off, I went to the bank. Quite a bit of snow was on the ground, and it was cold. While in the bank, there was a woman. She told the teller that her car wouldn't start, and she had to get a taxi to go home. I had nothing else to do and offered her a ride. She accepted. At the time, I drove a Volkswagen Beetle. When she came to the car, she said quite excited, "A German car, no, I will not set foot in a German car." People are different. You try and offer help and get beaten with a stick. You get over something like this—but it sticks in your mind. Suffern is located in Rockland County, an area which consisted of a population of approximately 75% Jewish ancestry.

Back in Suffern, I developed a hernia that had to be repaired before it gave me any serious problems. I knew that I had a hernia before I came to the United States. I had just been out of the hospital (fixing a hernia was more serious in those days), and on doctor's orders, I was to stay out of work for three to four weeks.

Harold Reder called me and asked if I could go up to Rochester to the Country Squire Inn, which was another one of his leased restaurants. I told him that I was supposed to be out of work for a few more weeks, but he said that I didn't have to work—just stick around and observe the operation. So, I packed all my things into a 4 X 4-foot U-haul trailer, put a hitch on my car, by then a 1959 Edsel, and off I went. This was my first "encounter" with a city, which later became my home in the United States.

I guess the next "installment" should be Rochester and beyond!

Love, Dad

- 3 -

SOME HISTORICAL EVENTS circle the globe and get recorded in books, but most accounts of history, like my father's recollection of coming to America for the first time, would die with him. He wrote it down. It is monumental, but not uncommon. Millions of immigrants took, and continue to take, a similar leap of faith. Each person discovers surprises, new people, fascinating places, possible prejudice, and—for many—a new home. My existence is based on that airline ticket. Small decisions of the past can have huge implications for the future. When my father wrote about coming to the United States and his earliest memories, he was seventy-five. He made the voyage when he was twenty-four.

Leaps of faith change the course of lives. There is no guarantee that a change will better a person's situation, but one thing is for certain: staying still and not moving at all is even more destructive. Even if my father's experience turned out to be disastrous, he would have learned, gaining knowledge and experience from the voyage. Making decisions and sometimes blindly taking a leap of faith develops hope and purpose. The consequences of faith can range from disaster to wild fortune, but learning supersedes both. Education creates awareness and guides people to understand the world around them and the life within them. Even rocky roads have street signs, and such it is with life. Taking chances and rolling the dice of our lives creates change. Hope and purpose are developed out of shifts in life. Drinking stagnant water will often make a person sick.

On birthdays in my fourth-grade classroom, we do a question and answer session with the honored student. They sit on a stool, and I quiz them about the day he or she was born. Knowing this is coming, most kids talk with their family about the day they were born the night before their birthday. Students that know their history look proud when they talk about it, even if the history is not perfect. I had one student recently tell the class about her birth and her mother's death shortly after. As shocking as it was, there is no changing that fact. Because the negative history was not buried by her family, acknowledgement and acceptance of this death came very early in life for this girl. It took a very brave family to put this approach in place, but had they not, the girl's discovery and development of hope and purpose in her life would have been further hindered by questions about her past.

As I continue to celebrate birthdays, I have noticed a trend. More often than not, children do not know what time of day they took their first breath, where their name came from, who was at the hospital, or what hospital they were born in. Twenty-five years ago, children knew their history and their ancestry. Now, I get responses such as "I *think* I am some Italian and Indian." People are letting go of history. It is not talked about as much. Our local antique dealer often tells me, "People don't care as much about the past as they used to." From the lens of a teacher spending days observing my life with fourth graders, I agree. It is heart-breaking—but it is also reversible. If you are a parent, a grandparent, or a relative, know that family history is a treasure chest of hope. Unlock it! Turn off the distraction, put away the cellphone, and see what is right there waiting to be recognized. Tell people about your history—your hopes and dreams, and even about the times you failed miserably. Unpack it all, like my dad did in his letter. If you fear judgement, suck it up and keep trying. Give hope a chance.

The development and discovery of hope and purpose may take a lifetime of work. It does not seem like much to pass along family stories, but the truth is, my father took the time at the age of seventy-five to write out his story of coming to America. His effort in private mattered. His gift, which I consider the single most important item I own, was his one-way ticket stub from Zurich to New York City dated December 2nd, 1959. He could have easily thrown it out upon his arrival, so why did he hold onto it? That ticket stub is the most tangible item I can hold and look at that represents hope and purpose. Each day, millions of airline ticket stubs are printed. This one represents the hard work and opportunities for my father prior to coming to the United States, and the proud journey he took has been remembered and passed on. He has given more than he has taken, worked hard, failed, succeeded, and has always thought of others first. He came with hope and purpose. We can't save everything, but we should try to save the things that matter. This Pan Am stub is worthless monetarily, but it is a priceless symbol of my father's discovery of hope and purpose.

The lifestyle of hope cannot be balanced with money. There is no association between the two; money is a distractor that causes blurry vision about what hope is. If people are to rediscover hope, this practice must end. Intrinsic rewards need to be embraced as the greatest gifts we can give to one another. Everything that is extrinsic in the end is just stuff.

Hope cannot be bought. The next time you have to give a gift, don't go to Walmart and walk aimlessly down aisles looking for something to fill a void or shop from your couch on Amazon. The reason so many people struggle with finding the perfect gift is that they do not know where to look. What people really need is a gift that helps them discover their hope and purpose. Often these gifts are free. Look in a drawer, a closet, or the attic. Brush off that piece of history that has a meaningful connection, write a note explaining its significance, and see what it can do for others. Then, go back to the mirror in the bathroom and see what it did for you.

Hope is contagious. At one point in my father's letter, he discusses contacting his friend, Leopold Schaeli, who was halfway around the world working in Izmil, Turkey. Today, formal interviews, second interviews, in-depth research, and so on would be done before a person takes a leap of faith based only on a letter. Skepticism kills hope. It mashes it like a trash compactor. In 1956, a simple letter from a friend and the honesty of a man's word gave a person hope because there were no distractions that allowed a person to distrust integrity. Could Leopold Schaeli have come to America only to be disappointed? Sure. But there was a lesser chance that failure would define the person. Had Schaeli come and things not worked out, hope would have saved him by not making this a crushing blow. Failures build and teach us if we let them, and our life's circumstances do not have to define us. The fear of failure shackles hope. Fear is poison to hope. If you struggle with hope, do you struggle with fear?

I was heartbroken when I first read about that Jewish woman refusing my father's offer for a ride on a snowy day just because he and his car were from Germany. My dad felt pressured to disguise his German nationality. He said that he came from Switzerland. Lying about who we are, whether it is done to remain humble, over a fear of judgement, or through an absolute lie about success or failure crushes hope. And the trouble with living this type of lifestyle is that once you have been dishonest with others, you will begin to be dishonest with yourself. Once in this snake pit, it is hard to survive. Honesty takes courage and may set a person back. Every person on this planet has an identity. Education and honesty about flaws and hardships should be worn with more visibility. Everyone has a gift to give the world. People with hope and purpose can identify their gifts and do not fear sharing them because they have not been stifled by naysayers who say it is wrong to live outside of conformity. Seize moments where you have the opportunity to give others the gift of your talents by internally and intentionally reminding yourself that, "I am damn good at that. This is why I was put on this Earth!" This act is not a conceited act if your strengths are used for the benefit of others.

If you are lazy, admit it, and make a commitment to make a habit out of working on something. There is joy in hard work, contribution, and citizenship. The challenge is to get through the first day when you decide to break a habit. Hope was in greater quantity in the post-World War II era. People were taking risks, willing to serve others, and starting over from scratch. Most people of that generation did not have a will because there was little to pass on. If they wanted something, they had to earn it. If something in their car or house needed to be fixed, the owner fixed it. There was pride in learning while working. My father's letter reveals how hard he worked. He essentially took orders from the owners, and he did not balk at any of them. When he was told that he was being moved to a different restaurant, he went. He worked hard, and this not only led to a sense of pride and a lot of great narratives about people he met along the way, but also produced a level of hope and purpose.

If you decide you want to have hope, you will need to decide that this is going to be a lifelong undertaking. The moment this maintenance is halted, hope and purpose will wilt like an unwatered plant. Grit is about having the courage to push through obstacles no matter what they look like because it is worth it. Grit means when nobody else believes in your dream, you still pursue your purpose. Whether we call it grit, hope, or resilience, the world is hungry for people to rediscover hope and purpose and share the joy and success that comes with it.

One final thought...

JUNE 5ᵀᴴ, 2017 WAS a rollercoaster. In February I had lost my mother to ovarian cancer. I woke up on June 5th and knew that it was the first birthday I was not going to be able to call my mom and apologize for getting a card late to her in the mail. I am not a procrastinator. I just buy something and never get to the post office. My mom always thought that was funny. June 5th, 2017, there was no mom to call. I barely cried when she died, but the tears were flowing that morning as I choked down cereal alone in my kitchen. Emotions are unpredictable.

Elementary teachers get a 40-minute "break" each day while the kids are at physical education, art, or music. It is not a break. I begin grading the mountain of daily work. This is also when I check my mailbox in the office. On a small sheet of paper in my box was a note that simply read, "call Dawn," with a phone number. It was an emotional spring. Four hours after I was pulling myself together in my car, I found out I was going to be the next New York State Teacher of the Year. It is the most conflicted I have ever felt in my life.

New York has a drawn-out process. The State Education Department lets you know in June that you will serve the following year. It comes with a warning. Under no circumstances was I allowed to tell anyone before the September Board of Regents meeting in Albany. That is when the New York State Teacher of the Year award is announced. Three months—nearly 100 days to sit on that kind of information. On June 5th, I only told my wife, dad, principal... and my mom, in my head.

Books always seem to have the dedication at the beginning, and this book is rightfully dedicated to my dad, Werner August

Albrecht. He wrote some of the passages in this book, after all. However, many of my thoughts in this book were ignited years ago by my mom. I have come to know her more and more though my own thoughts, actions, reflections, and the writing of this book.

Therefore, as an ending I dedicate this book to you too, Mom— everyone knew her as Margie.

A Word of Thanks:

As Peter Mehlman so perfectly advised, "Keep your brain open for business." Ten unique and wonderful individuals contributed their thoughts in the interviews. Thank you to Chris Lubkemann, Kathrine Switzer, Michael Warneke, QT Luong, Ken Deardorff, Peter Mehlman, Tom Osborne, Lawrence "Larry" Bacow, Beverly Cleary, and Monaj Bhargava. I gained insight, guidance, and contact information from National Park Service superintendent, Mark Engler. Much of this book was written while living on-sight at Homestead National Monument (renamed Homestead National Historic Park), and the environment was perfect for many late-night typing sessions. Thank you to Gordy Fox for his insight on biology. My son, Cory Albrecht, gave great ideas of people to interview. Thank you to my wife, Jenny, for supporting me as a sounding board. No doubt she has heard many different versions of each chapter. She and my daughter, Autumn, and Al and Brenda Cretney helped with the final edits. Thank you to Amy Green for fielding all my late night and early morning texts about the conventions of the English language. A shoutout to my editor, Sara Page. I have had the privilege to share ideas and gain feedback from the incredibly talented writer, Caurie Putnam-Ferguson. Her advice and positive actions were strong forces behind this book. Mark Pogodzinski is my publisher. I admire him for his service minded approach to publishing, allowing the author to enjoy the writing process.

Finally, my father wrote several sections of this book. He is a dedicated mentor and understands the importance of history. His contributions and dedication as a dad are immeasurable. A lifetime of gratitude would not even touch the surface.

About the Author

Christopher Albrecht has been a teacher for over a quarter of a century. He spent the first three years teaching in New Martinsville, West Virginia. Since 1998, he has taught fourth grade at the Fred W. Hill School in Brockport, New York. He is an adjunct professor at the College at Brockport. Albrecht is a graduate of St. Bonaventure University and Clarion University of Pennsylvania. Albrecht is the 2018 New York State Teacher of the Year and a 2019 Inductee into the National Teachers Hall of Fame. He is the author of <u>Unconventionally Successful</u> (NFB Publishing, 2020), and is the presenter of two TEDx Talks- "Dust and Sneakers, Crawling and Running" and "Giftedness for All." With a deep-rooted love for the natural world, its backcountry and education, Albrecht devotes his summers to the National Park Service. Albrecht lives in the town in which he teaches with his wife, Jennifer, and their beloved dog, Harley. They have three kids that are now adults: Autumn, Cory, and Aaron.

Made in the USA
Columbia, SC
10 July 2021

41676472R00159